Darcy,

Thank you for the Beautiful Music.

God Bless the St. Martin's Choir!

Dave Lahman

HOME
AT
LAST

a memoir

David H. Lehman

Edited by Greer Kann
Illustrated by Maddock Rigby

NEWMAN SPRINGS PUBLISHING
320 Broad Street
Red Bank, NJ 07701

First originally published by Newman Springs Publishing 2020

ISBN 978-1-64801-560-1 (Hardcover)
ISBN 978-1-64801-561-8 (Digital)

Printed in the United States of America

To Patsy
I love you forever

Contents

Acknowledgments

....

This book would not have been possible without our beloved daughter Lisa. She has been an invaluable source of information and assistance in writing this book. Lisa is the greatest joy of our life and has been a tremendous source of comfort to me over the last few years. She is the best part of the Three Musketeers.

My siblings, Roy J. Lehman II, Margaret Lehman and Tom Lehman, alongside Patsy's sisters, Sharon and Kathy, each read parts of the manuscript and provided not only valuable feedback but also encouragement for my efforts.

To Pat Broe of Denver, Colorado, who first introduced me to the concept of the gut-brain connection and the role of probiotics in brain health.

I would also like to thank Dr. Joan Fallon of White Plains, New York, who provided important criticisms on the research used in this book and whose own research has begun pushing against the unknowns of MSA.

This book is my memoir and reflects my recollection of these events. Some of my recollections may differ from others such as my siblings who were there at the time. I accept all responsibility for the telling and recognize that some things may be told differently than others remember. However, it is true to my memory and my thoughts.

Greer Kann

Greer Kann lives in New York City and graduated from Franklin and Marshall College. She currently works in human resources. She follows her true passion for writing and editing outside of work and hopes to one day make it her full-time profession.

Maddock Rigby

Maddock Rigby is an illustrator from Boulder, Colorado. Her medium of choice is linocut, a form of block carving. Each piece is hand carved onto a linoleum surface. The raised areas left behind from the carving are then inked over with a roller and pressed onto paper.

Prologue

....

The Southern Belle is an endangered species.

If you've never known one, let me try to describe her—but don't let my words fool you into thinking you've met one in real life. They are a true wonder to behold.

A belief in God and country, in that order, shapes the framework of a Southern Belle. A Belle's belief in a higher power centers and drives her to be a force of good. She becomes a beacon in whatever community she joins. Welcoming newcomers, raising money for a cause, and rallying other Belles behind a mission are all classic behaviors. Belles seek to help those who cannot help themselves, especially animals.

Loyalty weaves a strong base through this framework. Southern Belles are dedicated to their families and steadfast in their friendships. Sisterhood is particularly important to them, and they often have more male than female friends. Whether you are a friend or a stranger, a Belle will always remember when you helped them out and pay you back double.

Complementing all of this is a Belle's outsized appreciation of beauty and their friendly and outgoing disposition—unless provoked. Belles are exceptionally stylish, are well-mannered, and hold generally conservative views.

All of these items lend a Belle an air of constant purpose and composure. No two are alike, and I was lucky enough to have spent thirty-eight years and seventy-six days with mine.

Patsy Mayer was a perfectly unique Southern Belle who left me starstruck from the first time we met. Her sharp wit and warm smile took me in. Of course, as a man born and raised in Pennsylvania, a few miles north of the Mason-Dixon line, Patsy first had to convince her friends that the line swerved up around there.

Our decades together are one of the greatest blessings in my life. They were cut short when Patsy was taken from me by the ravages of a mentally and physically devastating illness called MSA, or multiple system atrophy, a severe form of Parkinson's.

This is the story of Patsy Mayer Lehman, our life together, and the unfortunate hell of the last years of her time on earth. Despite prayers, supplications, and the best medical advice we could find, I was not able to save her. In this memoir, I hope to capture the spirit of this feisty but eminently gracious woman.

PART 1

Daisy Duck and the Dutchman

1

Daisy Duck

The Mayer family story really begins in Ungstin, Bavaria, where, in 1824, Jacob Mayer was born. A German Jew, he decided in 1847 to migrate to Lafayette, Indiana. He married Barbara Hart, and the couple had six children together. Their third child was Max Mayer, Patsy's grandfather.

At thirty-four, Max moved to Little Rock, Arkansas, and spent several years working in the cotton industry. In 1895, Max Mayer and his partner Sterling Scott formed the Scott-Mayer Commission Company. It began as an import and distribution company, focusing on produce. As the years continued, the company expanded into a produce, dry goods, and merchandise distributor, becoming one of the largest in the state and a prominent fixture on the business scene in Little Rock. Max was president and the driving force behind its success, while Sterling provided all of the support as secretary and treasurer.

In 1902, Max Mayer married Daisy Dean. The couple had three sons: Jacob, Nicholas, and Theodore. Teddy, as his family and friends affectionately called him, was born in Little Rock, Arkansas, in 1914.

When Patsy was two years old, the family moved to Teddy's home-town of Little Rock, Arkansas, where they remained as the children grew up. The Mayer family settled at 1806 Battery Street in downtown Little Rock. It was an idyllic setting; a two-story home on a spacious lot, with a massive tree in the front yard and large porches with chairs for relaxing and watching all the neighborhood children play.

Patsy was greatly influenced by both Teddy and her mother, Robbie. Mary Virginia "Robbie" Mayer was born in 1916 in Talihina, Oklahoma; went to nursing school; and became smitten with the dashing Airman Teddy. Robbie had a strong Oklahoma small-town personality—friendly, outgoing, considerate of others; but it was her worldliness and feistiness that drew Teddy to her. There is no doubt that Patsy got Robbie's big, outgoing, friendly personality. They both had this wonderful ability to strike up a conversation with anyone, from CEOs to a clerk in the store, and make their day. The other trait she got from Robbie, for which I am continually grateful, was her loyalty and loving devotion as a wife.

Patsy adored Teddy, but she had inherited his stubbornness alongside Robbie's friendliness. They tangled on several matters over the years. Part of this stemmed from Patsy's role as the oldest sister. She felt compelled to look out for the interests of Sharon and Kathy, as much as or more so than for herself. Teddy had been raised in a very well-to-do, upper-class family in Little Rock, topped off by attending the Wharton School at the University of Pennsylvania. However, he was determined that his children be raised to appreciate their blessings, not lord their position over others, and be mindful of those less fortunate. He frequently said, "There but for the grace of God go I." Patsy accepted and appreciated this, but she thought that Teddy took it way too far. She chastised him for the family spending weekends at their farm outside Little Rock in lieu of joining the Little Rock Country Club, like many of her friends' families did.

As their downtown Little Rock neighborhood began to show signs of deterioration and economic decline, she begged Teddy to move the family to the suburbs, as many others were beginning to do. Teddy eventually did just that but years after when Patsy thought it should have happened. In his older years, one of the things that annoyed Patsy to no end was Teddy's insistence on wearing for just about any and every occasion, including when I first met him, his favorite bright red jumpsuit. He was not going to dress up for anybody!

Along with her parents, one of the persons who greatly influenced Patsy was her paternal grandmother, Daisy Dean Mayer, also known as Mimi. Mimi was married to Patsy's grandfather Max. They had lived in St. Louis, Missouri, for a time, where they ran a boardinghouse. Max and Mimi were somewhat secretive about their life prior to arriving in Little Rock; but one well-circulated rumor suggested that Mimi had a nervous breakdown when her oldest son, Jake, Teddy's brother, died at thirty-six as the result of a ruptured appendix.

When Max died, Mimi settled into a house just around the corner from Teddy and his family, so they saw her frequently. Although so close she was practically a member of the nuclear family, Mimi was generally not viewed by the grandchildren as a typical "warm and fuzzy" grandmother. The children loved her, but they were sometimes put off by her somewhat peculiar mannerisms. Sharon relates the story of how, when Kathy was born, although Mimi did not babysit frequently, the three Mayer children were sent to stay with her. According to Sharon, "Mimi sent us, accompanied by her maid, down to the neighborhood theater. Mimi popped popcorn herself and made us each take ours in a little brown paper bag rather than give us the money to buy some at the theater. It's not like she couldn't have afforded it. Patsy was a bit peevish about it. I can still see her face when Mimi handed her the bag! She was only seven at the time."

Nonetheless, Patsy favored Mimi in appearance and many of her mannerisms. Both of them also loved to cook and were excellent at it.

Again, Sharon recalls, "I remember being in Daisy's kitchen watching her cook in her apron. She would have chicken grease on her hands and smell slightly of garlic. This looked and smelled uncannily like Patsy, years later, as I watched her cooking in her own kitchen."

Another cooking anecdote about Daisy and a peek into her personality is a story relayed by Teddy. "Mimi was an excellent cook and could do wonderful things with food. She would sometimes cook a pork roast and send it down to the synagogue and tell them it was chicken. They couldn't tell the difference, and she showed no remorse whatsoever!"

Teddy had nicknames for each of his children, and none of them are sure what the origins of their names are. His son, Theodore, was Mike, Kathy was known as Ducie, Sharon was Terry Bear, and Patsy was Daisy Duck.

When Teddy came back to Little Rock after the war, he and his brother Jacob bought and ran the Black and White stores, a grocery store chain in Little Rock. However, in order to challenge his intellect, he also went back to school, got a law degree, and dabbled in real estate development. Teddy developed, more or less from scratch, a retail shopping center, which is at the corner of Rodney Parham Road and Markham Street in Little Rock. This not only provided a base of solid and secure income for many years but also was a source of pride for the family. Patsy would sit by Teddy's side for hours listening to how the shopping center was put together, and for her entire life, until her very latest years, she could recite from memory all of the significant transactions.

Teddy ran the grocery store chain, practiced law, and developed real estate; but he and Robbie both doted on their four children. Christmas was always a highlight, but perhaps none surpassed the Christmas of 1954. The children were at an impressionable age, Patsy being nine at the time. Imagine their glee when Santa Claus delivered two ponies right there in their front yard! Patsy's pony was black-and-white and was named Danny. Sharon's was brown-and-white and named Thunder. The mare Lady was for Mike but was left at the Mayer farm for this occasion. The ponies were taken to the Mayer farm and delivered many years of fun riding.

The religious life of the Mayer family was important but not overarching. For one thing, there were some confusing aspects to it. Teddy was part Jewish but raised primarily in the Episcopal Church, and Robbie was Southern Baptist. The children generally went with Robbie to Baptist Sunday school, church, and summer camps.

The family dynamics favored Patsy in some respects. As is the case in many families, Teddy put a lot of pressure on his oldest son Mike. Meanwhile, according to her sisters, Patsy was the model child who could do no wrong. Of course, they sometimes saw reason to report otherwise but generally kept it to themselves!

For example, the second story of the house on Battery Street was a large room with one bathroom at the back of the house. A divider separated the room so that Sharon's bedroom was on one side and Patsy's on the other. Patsy was apparently quite territorial and persnickety even at a young age and would chide Sharon for such seemingly minor indiscretions as walking on her newly vacuumed carpet! Sharon and Kathy totally did not know how to react when they discovered Patsy "the golden child," at the age of eleven, with two of her childhood friends—Pitsee and Lucy Jane—smoking cigarettes as they hung out on the second floor balcony so that their parents would not see them! On another occasion, as Teddy, Robbie, and young Kathy came home from a weekend trip to the farm, Robbie saw a blue Dodge on the other side of the road and said excitedly, "That looks like my car!" As it turned out, Patsy and

Lucy Jane, both fourteen at the time, had "borrowed" Robbie's car for a joyride!

Teddy's attitude toward money and education had undoubtedly been influenced by his experience of the Great Depression. Although the family came through the affair remaining one of the well-to-do families in Little Rock, they had made many changes to survive. Teddy's two older brothers, Jake and Nicky, had both gone to Culver Academy, the prestigious prep school in Indiana. By the time Teddy was ready to go off to school, the decline in the family reserves dictated a less expensive, less prestigious destination. It is difficult to know whether this experience left Teddy feeling defensive about not having attended the same institution as his brothers or whether as a result of it, he was left sincerely feeling that it was not necessary to spend extra money for a "name" school.

When it came to his children, he expected them to attend college but did not push them toward prestigious East Coast options. Although she mentioned it only rarely, this was another area in which Patsy felt that her dad had "overcorrected." In any event, Mike went off to Hendricks College, a small private school in Arkansas. For the three girls, the decision was more complex. Was there a thin residue of male chauvinism that made spending money on his girl's education less a priority, or was he genuinely concerned about the family savings as a holdover from the Depression? On top of this, Robbie wanted the girls to go to a women's college. As it turns out, the Mayer's neighbor across the street was Jane Gardner, the head librarian at the Mississippi State College for Women in Columbus, Mississippi (now called Mississippi Women's University). So the three Mayer girls, starting with Patsy, went off to "the W."

Patsy's recollections of the W were mainly the very strict rules about checking into and out of the dorms contrasted with tales of her dates sometimes driving to secluded concrete block "drive-thrus" to purchase bootleg liquor!

Patsy's high school sweetheart had gone to Columbia University in New York. After he graduated there, he enrolled at the University of Arkansas Law School. For her junior year, Patsy transferred from the W to the University of Arkansas so that they could be together.

Unfortunately, soon after school began in her junior year at the University of Arkansas, Patsy and "Mr. Right" broke up. It was a devastating event not only for Patsy but also for the entire Mayer family. Sharon recalls that it put her into a brief period of "hating men." The cause of the breakup, if there can be such a thing as a cause, is not known and was certainly never told to me. All I got were a few snippets shared indirectly that I put together, perhaps not even completely accurately. Patsy was a true patriot and intensely proud of her dad's service in the army during WWII. Whatever else may have transpired, she for sure was not happy about her friend's avoidance of military service during the Vietnam War.

Patsy was very disciplined in her studies at the University of Arkansas. One of her favorite places to study was the Presbyterian Student Center. She and one of her best friends, Martha Purdue of El Dorado, Arkansas, went there almost every day of the week, at Patsy's insistence. So despite the disruption in her plans, Patsy finished at the University of Arkansas with excellent grades and a degree in education. Upon graduation, Martha and Patsy decided that they would seek a faster paced life than they saw in Arkansas.

They considered Denver, Dallas, and Houston. They were leaning toward Dallas, but Martha's brother, Don, told them that Houston was a better choice because there were so many good-looking airline stewardesses in Dallas. Well, they thought, maybe we should be airline stewardesses. They checked into American Airlines and learned that Patsy was too short and Martha was too tall, so they decided to move forward with their plan to teach school in Houston.

Patsy and Martha each signed a contract with Houston Independent School District for a yearly salary of $4,800. They were originally assigned to separate school districts, but because they were roommates and hoped to carpool, they requested to be assigned the same school and were both placed at Briscoe Elementary in southeast Houston.

They arrived in Houston in June of 1967 and stayed with a friend of Martha's until they could decide where to live. Before the school year began, they had moved into their apartment at the Three

Fountains. At this time, they learned that HISD teachers had received a raise that would almost double their salary!

Having a huge raise they didn't expect, they thought they should celebrate by visiting a wig shop since hairpieces were in vogue. They met Lovice Brown, a Houston socialite, at the wig shop; and she took an instant liking to Patsy and Martha and took them under her wing. She gave them advice on everything—including men! She took them to lunch at the Warwick, which is now the Za Za, invited them to parties that included actresses, astronauts, and ambassadors, and became a lifelong friend.

Patsy and Martha took full advantage of the adventures the big city had to offer. They were outgoing and unafraid, creating new social circles and restarting their dating lives. Together they hunted, golfed, sailed, and partied—all of course on the weekends as they took their teaching very seriously.

Patsy taught second grade at Briscoe Elementary. She loved the students, who were mostly underprivileged. When a student was absent longer than a few days, Patsy would insist on going to their homes to check on them. She was always very focused on her teaching and the welfare of her young students. Houston had been the right choice, and Patsy taught at Briscoe for seven years before moving to a school closer to her apartment. She continued to love teaching in her new school but kept in contact and checked on former students.

One of Martha's great memories of Patsy included a date where Patsy had to go dove hunting. Hairpieces were still in vogue at this point, and on the dove hunt, Patsy's date held up the barbed wire fence for her to go under. As she came up on the other side of the fence, Patsy felt lighter and realized that her hairpiece had gotten caught on the barbed wire!

On another occasion, Patsy and Martha's dates took them to a driving range. Patsy was a natural and actually embarrassed the guys with her ability to hit the ball on her first try! This may have been a precursor to her great interest in golf later in life.

According to Martha, "Patsy was always popular and never lacked for a date, but when she met Dave Lehman, she knew she would never date anyone else. She had met the man she was going to marry."

2

Farm Boy

I grew up on a farm in southern Lancaster County, Pennsylvania. Luscious, green farm country—the Garden Spot of the World, it calls itself. We were Mennonites or "Pennsylvania Dutch." The Dutch description here is an Anglicized version of "Deutsch" or German. The Pennsylvania Dutch are largely descendants of Swiss and, in larger numbers, Germans who immigrated in waves to the East Coast of the United States in the 1700s. On my father's side, descended through his mother's lineage is one of the original German settlers in Lancaster County—Hans Herr, whose house is still a local tourist attraction.

The Mennonites originated in the Swiss-German area of Europe in the sixteenth century. Their namesake was a former Catholic priest named Menno Simons. Menno believed that scripture instructed that children should not be baptized until the age of conscious consent. Thus his followers came to be known as Anabaptists. The Anabaptists primary belief was the baptism of consenting children, but they also were against the taking up of arms—likely a consequence of the Swiss influence—Switzerland long having been a neutral country in wartime.

The Anabaptists were a very "decentralized" religion compared to the dominant Catholics of the time. As a result, each congregation, isolated in its own mountain valley, developed its own set of beliefs and practices. These customs were on subordinate issues such as dress and personal conduct invariably based on a literal interpretation of some verse in the Bible. As the groups migrated to eastern Pennsylvania, the landscape changed into an interesting, to say the least, array of different groups with different customs. One end of the spectrum would be the Amish, who reject all manner of modern convenience and are on their farms without electricity and driving their horse and buggies on the highway. At the other end, would be the Brethren, whom one could not easily distinguish from a Methodist or Presbyterian on casual examination. The Brethren do practice conscientious objection from wars and consenting child baptism. In between are other fascinating groups such as Old Order Mennonites, who resemble a cross between Mennonite and Amish. They use tractors but eschew rubber tires! Another interesting mix is the Black Bumper Mennonites. They drive cars but paint all of the normally chrome accessories black so as to not be accused of modern ostentation. The full array of these religious groups is on display even today in eastern Pennsylvania, most within a fifteen-mile drive of Lancaster.

For me the good and not so good of this entire culture is captured in two quotes: "German pioneers…were widely known for their industriousness, thrift, neatness, punctuality, and reliability in meeting their financial obligations" (Thomas Sowell describing the early German Settlers—many of them Mennonite—in Pennsylvania); and "They are hard on their horses, and harder on their women" (Sarah Anderson, a large-animal veterinarian in Pennsylvania and Ohio, describing current-day Amish farmers).

In the middle of this cultural milieu was the Lehman family of the Buck—our nearest small town. We went to the Willow Street Mennonite Church. A large brick and white wood building on the east side of the little town of Willow Street and essentially wrapped in large farm fields. Every Sunday, the Lehmans—Roy and Esther and their four children: David (me), Roy, Margaret, and Tom—would dress up in their "Sunday best" and go to church. The men would wear dark suits, white shirts, and a tie. Not just any tie, mind you, but a black bow tie, as a long tie, especially one with color, was deemed far too "worldly." This was our version of the "Black Bumper." The Willow Street Mennonite Church was founded in 1710, and I don't know if the black bow tie tradition carried on from the beginning or not. I suppose if something is working for you for three hundred years, there is no point in changing it. To this day, I wear a tie to church, but a long tie I've moved on!

Most of what I remember as a young boy going to church is fighting with my brother Roy in the backseat on the way there, listening to long sermons, and learning how to catch a short nap during the sermon—a talent which has stayed with me throughout the years.

One hundred and twenty acres. That was our farm. It was big enough to need a lot of work to operate but not large enough to generate much extra money. The Mennonites and Amish (or Plain People, as they were commonly referred to by their neighbors) were well-known for growing labor-intensive cash crops. Ours was a dairy farm. The cows had to be milked twice a day, 365 days a year. Other sources of income were tomatoes, hay, and tobacco. A great irony, the Plain People would listen to sermons on Sunday about not drinking or smoking but were among the largest growers of tobacco in Lancaster County. This was never explained to me as a young boy, and I confess that I did not ask. If it had been explained, I think my parents would have said something like, "The heathens are going to smoke anyway, so we might as well make the profits and give them to the Lord!"

I never felt either poor or unloved growing up. It was only later in life when I saw how some of the rest of the world lived that it even occurred to me to think about such things. Everyone I came in contact with seemed to live about the same—a nice middle-class lifestyle. More accurately, all the same class, as I only learned the concept of "middle class" much later in life, and I'm sure many in the actual middle class would have characterized us as poor.

The ubiquitous quality that we learned at a young age was hard work. This was ingrained as almost a religious belief, with perceived value in and of itself. In fact, I once overheard my dad talking with my mother about me and him, saying, "Yes, but he hasn't really learned to enjoy working yet." When my doctor today looks amazingly at X-rays of my hands and wonders how these could have developed I explain to her my early days. We both joke about how my upbringing might be considered and probably frowned upon in today's times. For example, my dad used to brag to his friends that his son Dave could "spear tobacco" (a backbreaking chore done in the hot sun of August) as fast as any man, when I was only twelve years old.

Another story I sometimes tell folks who ask why I am still working at my age is one my mother used to tell friends. I do not remember the incident itself, but I'm sure that my mother, a very godly and serious woman, would not make up something like this. One morning, my mom and dad got up at their usual 4:30 a.m. milking of the cows. When they came in after sunrise for breakfast, I came down from my second-floor bedroom to join them—but Davey Boy, as my mother frequently called me, was not happy on this particular morning. I threw a small tantrum and scolded them for not having awakened me when they got up so that I could go help milk the cows.

I was six years old at the time.

Open displays of affection were not readily apparent in the Mennonite community. It's not that they were banned; it is just that the tradition seems to have evolved in the opposite direction. At Willow Street Mennonite, the men sat on one side of the aisle (left looking forward), and the women sat on the other. A picture of Mom and Dad, taken soon after their wedding, shows them standing about six inches apart, small smiles on their faces, not holding hands. Christmas was, you might say, more recognized than celebrated. Mom would put a small string of lights on the little evergreen tree just outside the front door, and presents would be opened on Christmas Eve. One of the presents I remember most distinctly was a fresh orange. During the middle of winter in 1953, with snow on the ground and everything a bit bleak, a fresh orange to a young kid in southern Lancaster County was a delicacy.

Along with this lack of outward displays of affection was a very taciturn approach to matters of life and death. My cousins (of which there were many) would love to come to our farm to camp out, play in the creek, ride horses, and otherwise indulge themselves in many of the things which they did not have ready access to. One night, as we were camped out in a large tent, a strong thunderstorm came up. My cousin Jim stuck his head out of the tent and apparently got struck, or nearly struck, by lightning. He came back into the tent like a shot and spent a long time screaming, "I'm going to die. I'm going to die." Eventually, he calmed down, and we all went back to sleep not thinking much of it. About a year later, Jim died of cancer. I often wondered if there was a connection but, of course, just went about my business and didn't say anything about it. I certainly felt bad when Jim died, but crying would have been out of the question.

We always had dogs growing up. Mostly they were St. Bernards, of which we had two or three over the years. They were perfect for the wide-open spaces and cold snowy winters. We loved them, as they were great companions (of course we would not have said it that way). They were not allowed in the house, however. This was partly a practical matter; they would frequently get covered with mud and dirt from their wanderings into the woods, and, well, dogs were just not allowed into the house. When I was about twelve, our first St Bernard was getting old and infirm. At the time, I was quite taken with a .22-caliber rifle, which I had received for my birthday. One day, when it seemed like our beloved St Bernard could hardly even walk anymore, Mom said to me, "I think that it is time for her. Why don't you take care of that?" I knew what she meant and took our dog down to a remote spot at the far end of the farm, dispatched her with the .22, and buried her. That was the way it was done down on the farm. No time for tears.

The name of that first St. Bernard dog was Patsy.

We always had several horses on the farm. Occasionally we'd use them for light farmwork, but more frequently it was for recreation. We'd go riding on a Sunday afternoon or when we had guests. However, a favorite pastime was hitching them up and going for a ride in the "buckboard." A buckboard is the horse and buggy version of the pickup truck. It is a light one-horse wagon with a seat for two and the back open for hauling things. Mom and Dad had met at the dairy where they each had hauled milk from their respective farms for processing to be bottled and delivered to customers. Mom had the very same buckboard, which she had driven on those occasions. We had it painted a bright green with yellow stripes. One of our favorite horses to hitch to the buckboard was a huge sixteen-hands-high roan gelding named Rex. Rex was strong and could run faster than any creature for miles. He barely noticed the light wagon. We frequently gave guests a ride in the buckboard, and it was also a favorite at some of the family reunions held at the Lehman family farm at the Buck.

Quarryville was the nearest town of any size to the Lehman farm and where the high school was located. It was only about five miles from the Buck to Quarryville, but to a young boy of nine, it might as well have been a thousand miles. Every year, the town of Quarryville put on a fair with a parade. In the summer of 1955, it was decided that the history of milk transportation from farm to dairy would be celebrated. Dad and I would ride on the buckboard with some old-fashioned milk cans on the back, and one of our neighbors would follow behind with a new tractor trailer designed to haul a large bulk load of milk in the modern way.

On the morning of the parade, I was so excited as we got ready to hitch up Rex to the buckboard. The buckboard was there on the crushed stone driveway by the barn, right in front of a huge locust tree about ten feet in diameter. It was the middle of summer, and everything was lush and green, the corn about ten feet high. Dad decided that Rex should be brushed before being hitched up.

Unfortunately, no one could find the curry comb. A curry comb is a small brush used for the purpose of smoothing a horse's coat, commonly used after taking off the harness or saddle and before putting the horse to pasture or in the barn or in similar fashion before hitching the horse to pull a wagon or saddling them up. Generally, there were several of them lying in the tack shed, but on this morning, none could be found. We looked high and low—no curry comb. Dad decided that I was the likely culprit as he remembered me being the last one to brush down one of the horses. He was furious at the misplaced comb. Dad decided that the appropriate punishment was that I would just have to stay home and miss the parade. I thought that he surely was not serious; I had my heart set on going to that parade. However, I watched dumbstruck and in disbelief as he drove off to the parade without me.

I was devastated. Of course, I did not cry, because we did not cry down on the farm.

Needless to say, the punishment certainly seemed incongruent to the crime in this little boy's eyes, although I must say that I paid close attention to where I put the curry comb from that day on.

*****

The first lesson that I received in finance from my dad still sticks vividly in my mind. We were at the grocery store, and I don't remember what happened exactly leading up to this, but somehow I had negotiated with the clerk to pay only part of what I owed—i.e., fifty-two cents owed and I was going to just give him two quarters. Dad had overheard the exchange. "No," my father said quite sternly, "you must pay to the exact penny *and* get exact pennies in change as well." It really stuck, as even now I do not let the barista at Starbucks get a penny out of the jar to round things off but insist on paying the full exact amount. This is what stuck with me, for even though we did not have a lot of money; the money we had was counted carefully. In my whole time growing up in Lancaster County, I did not know, or even had heard of, anyone declaring bankruptcy. This would have been probably considered in the same category as a major capital crime in the minds of the Plain People.

*****

The yellow school bus—this was a big deal growing up on the Lehman farm. Neither Roy nor Esther had been to college, but they were determined that their children would have that opportunity. My father, who had been the oldest of twelve children, had not finished the sixth grade, having had to work on the farm to help support the family. Two of his brothers went on to get PhDs—a fact that I'm sure was a source of envy for him, although he never talked about it in that light or much at all in fact. The four Lehman children did, by the way, all get that opportunity and not only attended college but graduated and went on to successful careers in various areas.

The emphasis on education started early, and bringing home report cards for review was the first part of this process. My mother was always the more tolerant. I remember on a number of occasions showing a poor grade to my mother first so she would help me shield the bad news from Dad, who was not understanding in these matters. "Oh yes, Davey Boy had real good grades," would sometimes do the trick and meant that I would not have to show the actual card to my father—with the possibility of an unpleasant result. To be clear, the unpleasantness would come in the form of a scolding and/or additional chores assigned. Corporal punishment was not practiced in the Lehman family or in any of the other Mennonite families that we knew.

Although I did fairly well in school, I had a difficult time sitting still long enough to do homework, frequently leaving it to the last minute. Once again, my mom would frequently help me with my homework, and I remember on many occasions having to make the school bus wait while we both tried to get an assignment done—she sometimes typing out an essay or other such paper for me. For my brother Roy, this was a major source of irritation, although he only told me this later in life. Roy was the smart one, consistently got excellent grades, and was very conscientious about his homework. Mom and Dad decided early on that he should become a doctor, and sure enough, he eventually did just that. Roy would frequently have to sit on the school bus and beg the driver to please wait for me as I was "on the way." I would come tearing out of the house, running down the lane of about seventy-five yards to catch the bus before the driver got impatient and drove off.

On the occasions when the bus left without me, I would sprint across the cornfield (or whatever other crop might be in season) to try to catch it at the Longenecker farm stop, about a quarter mile down the road. When that failed, I would have to come back home and ask Mom to drive me to the end of Penny road, where the bus made a big loop, and we could wait for it to come back around. My mother was a kind and long-suffering soul, and she might have done me some good by letting me suffer the consequences of my tardiness by way of teaching me a lesson on the value of planning, but she *never* did!

Of course, all of the schoolwork and attendance had to be wrapped around the farmwork. I remember one day my high school math teacher, Elsie Tellford, a kind and pretty but very large lady whispering in my ear, "Dave, you have some cow dung on one of your shoes. Why don't you go to the bathroom and clean it off!"

As I entered high school, various new interests tempted me and started to cause my first disagreements with Mom and Dad. Mother, one of eleven children of a farm family, had grown up near the quaint little town of Lititz and remembered fondly listening to the Moravian trombone band every Christmas. Dad's youngest brother had been a brilliant musician but had tragically been killed in a car crash before the age of twenty. Wouldn't it be great if Davey Boy could play the trombone! The only problem was that Davey Boy couldn't figure out how to read music, had a tin ear, and hated band practice.

I wanted to go out for football instead. Dad thought it took too much time away from farm work in the critical fall harvest season. We butted heads for years until finally, in my junior year, I went out for football. Then I fell in love with wrestling and wanted to do that as well. Some of the other boys thought the practices were hard. To me, they were a lot easier than baling hay or hanging tobacco.

I am on a board with a friend of mine, and he occasionally says to me, "What I love about you, Dave, is that you'll bull your way through a concrete wall to get what you want." What I have never told him is that I had to bull my way through a concrete wall to get where I am. The wall's name was Roy Lehman Senior!

As I began my senior year in high school, my parents and I still entertained the idea that I would try to get into college. However, none of us had a clue on how to go about applying. We talked about it, but we might as well have talked about how to fly to the moon. Mom, bless her, tried to help me send off for some brochures and such, but I had never even been on a college campus and didn't know what to do. Finally, one day in February, after wrestling practice, I said to my wrestling coach, "Coach Hartman, could you help me get into college?"

Coach Hartman had wrestled at a local private college named Franklin and Marshall, named for the United States's founding father Ben Franklin and John Marshall, first chief justice of the US Supreme Court. My parents always thought Roy might go there, because it had a reputation as a good premed school. But Coach Hartman came through and put the wrestling coach Roy Phillips in touch with me. Within a week, I had a visit to campus. I had never even dreamed about such a place. The beautiful ivory covered brick buildings were preppy—and rich looking, to me at least—with students all scurrying about. There were all kinds of interesting-sounding courses to choose, and in another two weeks, I had an acceptance letter. I felt like I had won the lottery.

Davey Boy was going to college.

3

The Road to Texas

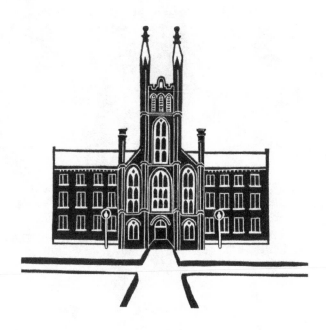

As excited as I was about the fall, it couldn't erase the trepidation filtering into Penny Road. My paternal grandfather's farm was less than a mile from Franklin and Marshall, and yet no one from the Buck Lehman family had ever been on the campus. To my parents and their parents before them, F&M was a playground for rich kids from New York, filled with fancy cars and fraternity parties. It was considered a den of hedonistic activity. A center for self-indulgence. The reputation of F&M's excellent premed program contrasted these thoughts enough that they still entertained the possibility that my brother Roy could attend.

Even with the tempering of its academic reputation, I distinctly remember my father taking me aside as we were walking out to the barn for work. "Now, Dave, you've got to be careful that those city boys don't lead you into things you shouldn't be doing." It was a statement broad enough to cover all of the possibilities I might come across on campus but lacked the advice I would soon need on how to deal with it all.

While my parents worried for my well-being, I worried about where I was going to come up with the money for school. It was pretty clear from the beginning this was going to be all up to me. Our 120 acres kept us going, but it produced no spare cash. My parents were simply not going to be able to help. The college had bent over backward to provide a package that would allow me to attend, and I was not about to allow the mere lack of money to stop me. Another concrete wall for me to bull through. As laughable as it sounds today, the tuition, room, and board for F&M back then was about $3,500 a year. I was supplied with scholarships, loan money, and the promise down the road of an on-campus job. I had saved some money working for our neighbors on their farms and, one notoriously hot summer, working part-time at the Buck Iron Foundry. The inside of that place must have been 120 degrees in the heat of summer.

When I looked at the situation, I knew that it was going to be a stretch. I decided I would commute my freshman year to save on rooming costs as F&M was only about a half-hour drive from the Buck. I would miss out on the famous college boarding experience and lose an extra hour every day, but I was determined to play football, wrestle, and get my degree. In today's environment, a good guidance counselor would have advised me against this, but I was on my own and had made my plan. Dad generously allowed me the use of his car and put my plans into motion. By my sophomore year, I arranged to stay in dorms at the Lancaster Theological Seminary across the street from campus. Although it did not have the same ambiance as college dorm living, it was cheaper and allowed me to keep working toward my goal. By my junior year, F&M worked out a dorm counselor job that gave me free room and board. It was a godsend.

In hindsight, this was definitely a better deal for me than for the college as I was probably one of the worst dorm counselors in the history of F&M. The younger students loved me, and that was the problem. I was so busy with class, homework, and sports that I really didn't have time to pay much attention to the residents. It was working out great right up until it didn't.

One night, I got back to the dorm late and found that the residents had created a swimming pool. They had dammed up the shower with two pieces of plywood along its edges and a plastic lining across the bottom to keep the water from draining away. After filling up their new pool up, the weight of the water, being far more than the normal weight of a college student, broke through the bathroom tiles and leaked all over the floor below. I, of course, arrived just as the dean of students had finished assessing the damage. Who knew those city kids were going to lead me into something like this? Fortunately, the dean only had a short talk with me, and afterward, I went about my business, never to hear any more about it. I always had the sense that everyone in the college was pulling for me, even after this little incident, and I very much appreciated it.

Besides dorm living, another facet of college life was to elude me. Although several fraternities rushed me hard, I decided not to join any of them. The guys could never understand my reasoning, but I had my feet in two worlds. I knew that my parents were very anxious about their son studying in this den of sin. I decided that I could relieve their concerns a bit by not getting involved in fraternity life. In keeping with the taciturn pattern of my upbringing, I never actually explained this to my parents. I just decided that this is was how I would handle it. The fraternity brothers never seemed to understand my choice, perhaps concluding that I was a bit off.

Looking back, I think there was another element involved in the decision not to join a fraternity. The whole atmosphere on campus intimidated me tremendously. Many of my classmates had fathers who were businessmen, professors, stockbrokers, and so forth. They knew how to hold a knife and fork, chase girls, have a good time, and seemed to have a level of sophistication that I had never been exposed to. These differences greatly influenced how I handled the situation, and considering all the other things on my plate, I believe it was for the best.

F&M was a pretty small place compared to the other colleges I might have picked. However, it always had a reputation as a rigorous academic environment. A 50 percent dropout rate was the norm in those days. The president of the senior class gave a speech on one of our first days on campus that began, "Look to your left, and look to your right—one of those men will not graduate with you." He continued and later in his speech said, "If there are ten reasons why you flunk out of this place and one of them was that you didn't want to be here in the first place, the other nine don't matter." These words stayed with me, but I knew I wanted to be there, and I was insistent on graduating—with or without the men standing next to me. There were no support groups for first generation students or other avenues to seek help back then. I was determined to succeed and made my own calls along the way. My sports teams and later my chosen major of geology provided support and structure that were critical in helping me graduate.

I was prepared to make whatever sacrifices were necessary to graduate, but after having had to fight so hard to get the chance to play football for the last two years at high school, I was not about to sacrifice sports.

The freshman team kicked off with two-a-day practices in the hot August sun a few weeks before the semester began, providing a nice lead-in to college. I liked the coaches and the other members of my team and began to find my place in their company. Williamson

Field, where we practiced, was plush compared to Solanco High School and continued to feed my exuberance at having won the lottery. During preseason, the Lancaster paper ran a large photo of the F&M freshmen from local high schools, and there I was, my picture in the paper on top of everything else!

One of the freshman coaches was Dusty Ritter. He had been a legendary player at F&M and held many passing records. After teaching high school for a while, he returned to Princeton to get his PhD in geology. His full-time job was as a geology professor at F&M, but because of his love of the game, he volunteered as an assistant football coach. Dusty was a tremendously likeable guy: jovial and easygoing with a huge smile and hearty laugh. He loved the game, the players, and his students.

About a month into the season, we were chatting after football practice, I still in my pads and he in his coach's attire. He asked me what I was thinking of majoring in. Having just started to figure out how to balance my week-to-week schedule, I hadn't quite thought about the rest of it yet. I told him I was thinking about a math major but hadn't set my mind to anything yet. He suggested that I try geology, and this put me on a path that truly changed my life.

In the second semester of my freshman year, I signed up for Introductory Geology. I was hooked. It was the perfect combination of science and outdoor activity. The farm boy found his home. To make it even better, the course was taught by the head of the department, a guy equally as likeable as Dusty: Professor John Moss. A tall, thin man with a crew cut, he had a booming voice and, like Dusty, a ready smile.

Professor Moss always greeted each student by name. The only issue with me was he kept calling me Jim. He was so friendly and avuncular I just went along with it. For at least a year after my entry into the department, he called me Jim. Finally, one day I said, "Dr. Moss, why do you always call me Jim when my name is Dave?" He didn't miss a beat and with a big laugh said, "Well, you are always down at the gym, so to me, you are Jim."

Transitioning from the Buck to F&M was a tremendous challenge, but the freshman wrestling team proved to be one of the strongest support systems for my transition into college life. I went about freshman year just like I did working on the farm—keeping my head down and plowing ahead, not giving too much thought to the situation at hand other than my role in "getting the job done." Wrestling, more so than football, gave me an on-campus community. Its time commitment forced me to balance academics and sports rather than continue bulling my way through and hoping for the best as I had been doing throughout football season.

In those days, freshmen were not allowed to compete on the varsity team, so we had a separate team and our own schedule. It was a challenging schedule against what are now called Division I opponents such as Lehigh, Temple, Bucknell, Harvard, Columbia, and so forth. I loved the sport. It gave me a great opportunity to socialize with my teammates, many of whom were from different, often more sophisticated, backgrounds. We got along well, and I developed fast friendships. However, we brought our backgrounds to college with us, and I remember an incident which has haunted me to this day.

I was living at home that year, and our freshman coach, Bob Getchall, was a hard driver. Roy Senior would have been proud of him had they known each other in different circumstances. Getchall was younger than varsity Coach Phillips but not at all as personable. He pushed us hard and maintained this intense look on his face, like he was always figuring out how he would pin you. During my season, he implemented a regular practice on Sunday evening. Well, Dad wanted to know why I had to take the car out on Sunday evenings, and I knew that he would not have approved of this departure from the Sabbath Day edict to rest from work (milking cows an obvious exception!). So when he pressed me on this, I told him that there was a "youth meeting at the church." Not even the Commandments were going to deter me from achieving my goals.

Coach Getchall's work ethic and our dedication paid off, as our freshman wrestling team went undefeated. We were all so proud of the accomplishment, and that season has stayed with all of us to this day.

I ended up playing football and wrestling all four years at F&M, going varsity on both after my freshman year. No good mentor would recommend such an ordeal, but my decision to play both sports for all four years was not a strategy thought out ahead of time. The opportunities presented themselves, and I couldn't, or bullishly wouldn't, say no. Football started with its "two-a-days" in the summer, and in many ways, this was a break for me. It was far easier than the summer jobs I could have been doing. I loved the collaborative aspect of football and the challenge of pulling the whole team together. Our coach, George Storck, was a former army officer who had lost two brothers in the Korean War. With his crew cut and erect bearing, he certainly cut a military-looking figure. I respected him deeply. He was a kind man with a no-nonsense attitude on the field, "Stand up, no sitting on your helmets!" I could easily relate to Storck's discipline as I had, after all, been raised in a religion of no-nonsense.

The wrestling conversation occurred on the first Monday after the last football game of the season. It happened every year of my college career, and I doubt there was more than ten words difference in any of them. Organized wrestling practice would have already started. It would invariably be a beautiful fall day, and at about four in the afternoon, I would finally get up the nerve to go see Coach Phillips. He had the look of a man larger than his immediate place in life. Sitting behind a modest wooden desk, there were pictures of all sorts surrounding him: of his wrestling teams, and with well-known people, perhaps a famous coach or the president of the college. Coach Phillips would be sitting with his back to the window, the fall foliage and beautiful brick buildings of the campus creating a remarkable background. He sat there with his warm smile in invariably casual but very neat apparel. A brown sweater over a checkered shirt gave him the look of an outdoorsman just waiting to swap a good story.

"Hey, Coach, thanks for seeing me."

"Of course, Dave—what can I help you with?"

"Well, you know that I've just finished up with football. My ribs are sore, and my ankle is still hurting. I'm a bit behind in my schoolwork as well and could really use some extra time to study. How about I take off a month or so and come out for wrestling around the first of the year?"

The whole time the smile rarely left his face, and he leaned forward, listening intently to every word I said. It was quiet, only a few birds chirping outside the white wood and glass-paneled windows.

"Well, Dave, you know that I really need you at the hundred-seventy-seven-pound weight class."

Wrestling practice started at 6:00 p.m. Of course I was there. Coach Phillips had gotten me into college. The farm boy couldn't say no. The wrestling room was a seventy-five-square-feet concrete-block windowless room with a wrestling mat on the floor. Many days during the season, I would feel like quitting, overwhelmed by one or other of my commitments, but I never did. Walking bullishly forward.

And so it went for four years.

Coach Phillips maneuvered the line up to give us what he perceived to be our best chance of winning the match. For the first few years, this involved throwing me to the wolves. He determined that none of his wrestlers would be able to beat Dave Schram from MIT, so he had me wrestle him in the hopes that the other guys would win some of the lighter weights. My job was to stay off my back, avoiding a pin. I was able to do this most matches, not that that kept me from losing but at least postponed it for a few more moments.

After four years of fighting each other, Dave Schram and I became friends after college. Several years later, when I arrived at the University of Texas at Austin for graduate school he had a teaching job in the Astronomy Department. He was a renowned young astronomer who had already won several prestigious awards. In addition, he had started up a wrestling club and recruited me to join. Wrestling was not as big a sport in Texas as it was in the northeast, so I was a star! Dave was also a licensed pilot by this point. He flew his own plane and, a few years later, died in a crash while flying solo on a cross-country trip. It was a true shame that the world lost such a talent.

*****

Enthusiasm for my geology major only grew after the first course. Each class made me reexamine the world around me. I remember learning about the intricacies of the Susquehanna River, which ran not far from where I had grown up. I learned how it formed, the unique geological formations that directed its path, and how it was directed by slow erosion. I was captivated by the idea that the world could have so many systems happening around me.

One of my favorite professors was Don Wise, a wiry man with disheveled hair, seemingly endless energy, and a burning enthusiasm for structural geology, which is the study of how rocks fold and break. On many a Wednesday afternoon, structural geology lab would run overtime, and we would end up using the headlights of the department van to illuminate on whatever "nuanced" outcrop Professor Wise was lecturing about.

The professors led many field trips. They created a culture of infectious love for what they were doing. I was one of a group of students happily smitten with it and sought every opportunity to enjoy their knowledge and camaraderie.

One of the most memorable trips we took was to Georgia over spring break. I was with a couple other geology majors who also played football with me. We stopped at an all-you-can-eat fried chicken place for lunch, and they ran us out of the place for fear of losing their entire inventory!

In addition to my enthusiasm, I seemed to have a knack for the topic, and my grades got better as I went along. I began taking geology-related jobs during summer vacation. The summer after my sophomore year, I obtained, with the assistance of my professors, a job with the United States Geological Survey. My boss, a noted glaciologist, was working on a project mapping the glacial history of Yellowstone National Park. Glaciers had overrun the park at least four times in the recent geological past, and he was seeking to map out the extent and size of the glaciers for each period. We went into the backcountry of Yellowstone, far from what any tourist would see. Every Monday, we each set out with two riding horses to rotate and our own packhorse to hold provisions for the week. We would set up a base camp and work from there, generally riding our horses to even more obscure locations.

My job for the summer was twofold: take care of the horses and help dig the trenches to examine the glacial soil. Taking care of the horses was natural for me; I loved helping feed and tend to them during the week. Digging was also no foreign task for me, and I rarely minded doing it.

The most memorable event of the summer had little to do with our geologic work. As we were out scouting various geologic sites, we came to a steep, rocky ridge. We knew it would be too hard on the horses to ride them up, so we dismounted and began leading them up to the peak of the mountain. As we came onto the peak, there was a flat area maybe two hundred feet in diameter. Directly across from us was a mother grizzly bear with her two cubs. The horses spooked pretty badly, and I couldn't keep hold of mine, so he ran away. My boss's horse was gentler, and he managed to hold him, quickly climbing into the saddle and telling me to climb on behind him. I happily acquiesced. So there we were, two scientists on a horse, staring down a grizzly bear and her cubs! I was familiar with the way horses reacted when they were angry or threatened. They bare their teeth and lay their ears back. After a short while and without any prodding from either of us, our horse unexpectedly bared his teeth, laid back his ears, and charged straight at that grizzly bear! She chased her right off the plateau. It was an exciting moment that neither of us was looking to experience again.

Back at F&M, my junior year commenced, and I was rocking along with As and Bs until I signed up for advanced calculus, a requirement for the geology major. It was a difficult course for everyone, but I had become overconfident and a bit too nonchalant. I remember thinking, "Oh well, he will have to grade on a curve because of all the low grades students were racking up." The calculus professor was, in my mind, a typical nerd with no personality, and I found it impossible to communicate with him. Imagine my shock at the end of the semester when the grades came out and I was given a big fat F. I had never experienced such a thing. I was eventually able to retake the course and earn a B (from a different professor), getting myself back on track.

My professors began to suggest that I had the capacity for graduate school and should perhaps even aim for a doctorate in the subject. This was heady talk for me that I might aspire to be one of them! As my senior year approached, my professors thought they had the perfect place for me to go. Several other F&M geology students had gone to the University of Texas at Austin, or UT, with good results. I had never been to Texas, and I was excited about the opportunity.

For my senior project, I worked on a joint mapping project of rural Lancaster County. I worked with another student, and we focused on mapping the folds in Conestoga limestone. Once classes had ended and I had presented my final project, all that was left to do was wait for graduation.

Dusty Ritter, my football coach and the man who had gotten me to take a geology course during my freshman year, was a tremendously popular professor. He studied geomorphology, the science of water erosion, beach formation, and so forth. My friend Grant Skerlec, another Pennsylvania farm kid, and I got the idea that it would be fun to make Dusty's office into a "beach." We took the furniture out of his office, put down black construction tarps, laid down a pile of sand for a shore, and filled it with about a foot of water. For our finishing touch, we put in a live duck to swim in the water.

The duck was captured from the Risser's farm, just down the road from the Buck. My youngest brother Tom recalls how he dutifully followed his older brother's instructions to go to Mrs. Risser, a grumpy old lady, and get her permission to borrow one of her ducks. Upon discovery, the "duck pond" gained quite the attention on campus, even getting a picture in the Lancaster paper. Some suspected my involvement, but I stayed quiet. Upon finishing the chore, we realized it was an even bigger feat than we originally envisioned, and it occurred to us that some might consider this vandalism. Thankfully, the head of the department, Professor Moss, thought it was great fun and probably saved our hides from what would have been a far less forgiving college administration.

The years I spent at F&M were some of the most formative years of my life. The farm boy had entered knowing a whole lot about cows and fields and far less about the world outside the field fences. The education and friendships that F&M fostered set me up to handle much of what the rest of life was going to throw at me. For now, though, I had bulled my way through college and was off to continue this method in Texas in the fall.

PART 2

God and Country

4

Bucking the Tide

I was scheduled to enroll as a geology graduate student at The University of Texas at Austin for the fall semester of 1968. This was a brand-new level of opportunity for me; so in my usual manner, rather than resting up, I took a job that summer with the United States Geological Survey in western Montana. I looked forward to making some money and would enjoy being outdoors. We were in remote mountains, and I had not even bothered to give my forwarding address to the post office for the summer. It was my way of getting away for a while, doing what I enjoyed, working in the mountains, learning more geology, and not having to think about any real meaty subjects before the grind of graduate school.

Despite my best efforts to avoid them, world events were about to tap me on the shoulder. During my sophomore year at F&M, the Vietnam War began to intensify. The US Marines invaded Da Nang, and the need for more troops began to increase significantly. Young men were required to register for the draft at age eighteen. My eighteenth birthday occurred November 1964 during my freshman year at F&M. I went to the Lancaster draft board and registered as a conscientious objector.

This was not only my right but was expected of me. I was a Mennonite, and Mennonites registered as conscientious objectors—no questions asked. During my years at F&M, college students were given deferments, and so at first, the war was mainly in the background. But each year it escalated: more troops were needed, more men were drafted, and the US continued to struggle in Vietnam. In 1967, my junior year, there was talk of ending deferments for graduate students—a major departure from past practice. This, of course, got the students' attention, and during 1967 and 1968, there were antiwar protests on campuses all over the United States. The Tet Offensive of 1968 took a tremendous toll on American lives and greatly increased the need for more troops, increasing opposition to the war even more. During my senior year, students at F&M took over and shut down Old Main, the main administrative building on campus, in protest.

Davey Boy had a dilemma. As I entered the second semester of my junior year and the start of my senior year, I had to at least consider the war, which was haunting just about everyone. I was really enjoying my new life. If I were to get drafted, how did I feel about being a conscientious objector? I struggled with this interminably. Sports gave me a good physical outlet to get things off my mind, but it was hard to focus on the matches. Most of my classmates were thinking about how they were going to game the system to get out of the draft. It made me feel like a fool to mention that I was considering whether I could in good conscience remain a conscientious objector. A friend suggested I shouldn't feel this obligation while a professor suggested that I should go if called and to just look at it "like getting a tax bill." Easy to say if the tax bill is coming to someone else.

There was tremendous uncertainty about what would happen. Would the war be over in a year? Would deferments be reinstated? What would one's local draft board do? My sense of patriotism and duty won out. I decided that, if called, I had had the benefits of living in a great country and I would do what she called on me to do. In the back of my mind, I believe there was another consideration. I never mentioned it to anyone and, in fact, have never stated it until now. In high school, I had learned about the Second World War and the sacrifices citizens made. Deep down, it always bothered me that my father had spent the war years on what were essentially work projects designed for conscientious objectors. In my mind, I didn't think they made any real contribution to the country.

Ultimately, the most difficult part was telling my parents. Despite our differences, I loved them dearly. I knew this was going to break their hearts, though they would never show me. I had a number of discussions trying to explain my view—including some heated exchanges with Dad. Damned if I did, damned if I didn't.

Before graduating from F&M, I went down to my draft board and reversed my conscientious objector status. Rev. John Brenneman of the Willow Street Mennonite Church gave me a call and invited me to lunch. Reverend Brenneman was a tall and solidly built man; in another life, he might have made a great linebacker. He was a farmer, well-read, and extremely kind. He didn't try to change my mind. He just said the rules dictated that this action meant I could no longer be a member of the church. He assured me, though, that I would be welcomed back at any time if I changed my mind. I left with tremendous respect for the guy but knowing that I had left that world for good.

I left for Montana in the summer of 1968 not oblivious to the events of the world but not really knowing what to do about them either. It was kind of like that calculus class—hoping for a curve to help us all.

*****

I rolled into Austin, Texas, in late August of 1968. It was a typical late summer day for Austin. As I got out of my car and stood in the sweltering heat looking at the endless, desolate flat terrain, I wondered how I was ever going to last here.

As seeming proof that an ostrich can only keep its head in the sand for so long, about two weeks after I arrived in Austin, I got a message through the university's geology department from a former professor at F&M, Dr. Marvin Kauffmann. Marv had also come from the Plain People. "Please tell Dave that he has been listed in the Lancaster Paper as a draft dodger, not having responded to his draft notice sent out this summer." Perhaps I should have left a forwarding address after all. I wasn't sure what to do next. On cue, a day or two after I discovered my new status as a draft dodger, a second notice arrived for me in Austin: "Congratulations, you have been selected to serve your country."

The chair of the geology department at UT was Dr. Muehlberger, a burly Marine Corps reservist. I went to see Dr. Muehlberger and explained my situation. Muehlberger knew his way through the system. He turned around and picked up the phone, dialing the phone number for my draft board. I heard his side of the conversation as he explained what a great contribution Dave would ultimately make to his country if he could just finish his degree in geology. Unfortunately, the Lancaster draft board was short of bodies. They explained that since I was enrolled, I could finish out the semester, but after that no ifs, ands, or buts, I was going to be drafted.

I was hell-bent on getting that doctorate, just like my professors at F&M, but I decided that my first semester of graduate school was unlikely to result in a stellar performance with this weighing on my mind. I wanted to get it over with. I packed my bags and headed for army basic training at Fort Dix, New Jersey. I remember nothing of my drive from Texas back to the northeast as my decision suddenly hit me. Everything might not be okay.

Basic training was another new experience for the Lancaster farm boy. It was a mixture of Kentucky hillbillies, inner city kids, and college graduates like myself. It was weeks of forced marches through the sandy soil of New Jersey, singing bawdy army songs in cadence, led by masochistic army sergeants determined to find something wrong at every turn. I must admit they did not pick on the college boys as much as they did on the hillbillies. One Friday, Sergeant Garcia was selecting people for weekend KP (kitchen police for you civilians!). He was standing right in front of me—a bad move on my part. Of course I tackled KP with my usual vigor and by Sunday afternoon had huge blisters all over my hands and forearms from having had them in the hot water for a day and a half. A friend's parents came to visit that same weekend and looked at my hands worriedly, wondering if the same thing was in store for their son.

On another occasion, I got a weekend off and went to visit my friend Grant Skerlec, of duck pond fame. He had gotten into

Princeton (not being burdened by any Fs in calculus!). At the height of the Vietnam War protests, I bravely set off across the Princeton campus in my army dress uniform to find him. Grant was worried about getting drafted and had looked into enlisting in the air force, but it required a four-year commitment. Unbelievably, I advised him against doing it. I said, "Grant, four years as an enlisted man will rot your brain. Just get through it and get it behind you as soon as possible." Here I was, about to go into harm's way but still unfazed by the danger because I was only focusing on my mega-goal of that doctorate in geology. About four months later, I got a letter from Grant:

> Dear Dave,
> I followed your advice and got drafted. I am writing this letter from inside the latrine, because here at Fort Bragg the Marines do not allow us to write letters at all.

The war situation had gotten so bad that they were drafting people directly into the Marine Corps. As it turns out, Grant and I both went to Vietnam but each in the parlance of the day "came home with all fours."

After Fort Dix, it was on to Signal Corps training at Fort Gordon, Georgia. I was trained in all aspects of army communication, including the teletype machine. Of course, to be effective at teletype, we had to know how to type. The army had a solution for that: we sat every day in a wooden walled classroom with about fifteen typewriters set up in stalls. Instructions were posted on a screen in front of us, and tests were given at regular intervals. After eight to ten hours a day for two weeks, presto, we could each type at least thirty words a minute, a skill which I am using even now as I knock out the draft of this book.

At the end of signal corps training, the next duty station lists were posted by stapling a piece of paper to the side of one of the ubiquitous wooden buildings at Fort Gordon. A few each to Japan, Germany, and Korea. The longest list by far was for Vietnam. David H. Lehman was on that list. I was posted to leave for Vietnam in late May of 1969, just over six months after I had left Austin. A few friends met me at my parents' farm for a send-off. My mother was petrified and covered her fears by not talking much at all. Dad, as much as we had butted heads on the matter, stuck out his thick weathered hand and said, "Well, Davey Boy, good luck." I know that it was a difficult gesture for him.

*****

The flight to Vietnam landed in Anchorage for refueling and then on to Saigon. In the barracks in Saigon that first night, there was no doubt that I had come to a war zone. Rocket, mortar, and artillery fired all night long, clashing with the constant drone of helicopters around us.

I finally ended up at an artillery base camp in the mountains west of Nha Trang. They were low-rounded mountains covered with jungle, and our camp had been carved out of the wilderness. When I went back to visit decades later, the area had been completely overgrown again. First Field Force Artillery was the official name of our unit. It was my job to take tactical information from the forward observers and adjust the large 105 and 175 mm howitzers, which we usually fired twenty-four hours a day. I did not see a lot of frontline combat, as would be the case with an infantry or armored unit. We pulled guard duty on the perimeter at night, and Charlie naturally considered us a problem; so we frequently took incoming rocket, mortar, and small-arms fire. Unfortunately, some of these projectiles found their mark, and we had casualties. We developed a fatalistic attitude about the entire thing, as being in the midst of rocket or mortar fire is a bit like standing in a field during a thunderstorm: if you can hear it explode, it missed you.

One of the most unusual incidents, and perhaps even funny if it did not have such a potentially disastrous outcome, was a friendly fire scare.

We slept in what we called hooches. They had a tin roof, board slats halfway up, and screen the rest of the way. The floor was a hard concrete-like substance. The beds themselves were standard army cots, canvas with wood struts holding it all together. A single light-bulb with a single switch provided light in the nighttime.

We were generally on duty twelve hours, off twelve hours, seven days a week. The eight of us assigned to a hooch had the same shift interrupted only for tours of perimeter guard duty (four hours at a time pulled during the off duty hours).

Our base was separated from the jungle with just a wall of sand-bags and a roll of concertina wire at the top. For protection, we carried our M-16s with us at all times—always loaded with only the safety on. They were with us in the mess hall, on duty, or in the latrine; and when we slept, the M-16 was under the cot.

One night, around 2:00 a.m., we were abruptly awakened by the lightbulb being turned on. A black soldier was standing by the door. "I'm going to shoot all you white guys," he said. I hadn't noticed that we were all white guys in that hooch, but he obviously had. There were six of us there at the time; two were away on guard duty. The guy by the door was jumpy, and his speech was a little slurred, obviously drunk or high or both. My immediate thought was whether or not I could reach my M-16 and shoot him before he shot all of us. Being only two cots away from him, I could see that the safety on his weapon was off, meaning that in less than a second he could be spraying the hooch with rounds. It was scary—and I remember thinking, "*Damn*—after all that work, here I am, going to get killed by my own guy!"

I decided that the sudden movement of going for my weapon would likely end badly. Several of us had the same idea—let's talk him out of this: "Where are you from? Why are you so upset?" We talked and talked and talked. A real bunch of hostage negotiators with no training! After about an hour, he began to sober up. In another half hour or so, he became much more lucid and I think realized what he had almost done. Eventually, we talked him into giving up his weapon, and someone ran to get the military police. The MPs took him away, and we never heard what ultimately was done with him.

I did not want to be overconfident, but about halfway through my thirteenth-month tour, I began to feel pretty good that I would be going back to Austin. Sure enough, by late June 1970, I was on a flight back to Fort Lewis, Washington. On arrival, I was told that the army apparently did not need any experienced artillery aimers in the States and I was free to go. My military career had lasted a year and a half, and I had all fours.

*****

The spread of Communism was a real threat to the world and to Southeast Asia during this time. I firmly believe that US efforts in Vietnam definitely slowed the growth of this cancer and played a positive role in allowing regional victories in other countries. Public statements by leaders such as Lee Kuan Yew of Singapore and Malcolm Turnbull of Australia have suggested this. In Yew's memoir, *From Third World to First*, he talks about how America's efforts allowed for Southeast Asia to prepare themselves to stand up to Communism. Yew believed that Communism would have spread if the United States never did anything. I am proud that I had the courage to do what I believed was the right thing, and I am thankful that I came home pretty much none the worse for wear.

As I returned to The University of Texas at Austin in the late summer of 1970, I can tell you one thing for sure: Austin looked like heaven to me.

5

The Rooster and Roses

Standing behind the bar, I pulled the tap on the keg of beer and was totally mesmerized by the beautiful woman on the other side of the bar. She had asked me for a glass of beer, and I couldn't turn away from her gorgeous, large blue-green eyes.

I had seen her throughout the evening and noticed how she moved through the room entering conversations easily and walking around to greet all the people she knew. Her smile caught my eye, but it wasn't until she walked up to the bar that I noticed how beautiful her eyes were. They changed colors in different light, and the depth behind them fully captured my attention.

I lost track of the glass as it filled up and only pulled back as beer began to run over my hand and flow across the bar. She told me that her name was Patsy Mayer.

It was early in the summer of 1976. I was single in Houston and had just started working at Exxon. I was getting over a failed marriage and determining that I would never put myself in such a position again. I wasn't sure exactly how I intended to accomplish that, but in my young mind, I felt that it meant there would be no more marrying for me!

In my spare time, to clear my head and satisfy apparently unsated jock instincts to run around and tackle people, I joined a rugby team. Even in those early days, Houston was becoming a fairly cosmopolitan city with an eclectic range of activities and folks of all sorts from around the country and the world. Rugby was it for me, though. I thoroughly enjoyed the sport and the camaraderie of my mates on the team. One of the guys, Gale Borden, a well-off member of a storied Houston family, had purchased a small house on the east side of Memorial Park, where our rugby pitch was. The team, friends, wives, dates, and even sometimes our opposing team, would commonly meet there after a weekend match to drink and tell stories. It was dubbed the Rooster and Roses, and when it got rowdy, I wondered if this was what I missed in fraternity life back at F&M.

Patsy was Gale's date that evening, and I had seen them together at the matches for several weeks in a row. My honor would not allow me to steal a teammate's girlfriend, so I waited to see what would happen. Several weeks passed during which I noticed Gale coming to matches alone. I called Patsy.

Our first date was at a small Italian restaurant near the center of Houston called Michelangelo's. We had a wonderful time. Patsy had a way of getting me to engage in casual, lighthearted conversation, which was something I rarely did and sorely needed. Mennonite upbringings really stick with you. We began seeing each other regularly and exclusively. I would frequently go by her apartment on Sunday evenings to catch up and just talk. I was totally taken with her. She was one of the most stylish dressers I had ever met, and in those early days, she frequently sported a pair of maroon leather pants that made quite a statement. She also had many down-to-earth habits that I found extremely calming.

On Sunday evenings, she had a routine of doing her laundry and cleaning her apartment, and we would visit as she assiduously went about her chores. She would tell me about her family, her dad's service in the war, the shopping center in Little Rock, and perhaps most endearing, about the kids she taught in her school. Patsy loved her kids, and they evidently loved her back. In her apartment was a large flowerpot, colorfully painted in a patchwork quilt pattern, on which all the kids in a recent class had signed their names. Many of her students came from poor backgrounds and troubled homes. She would talk to me about her attempts to intervene when she suspected abuse and most strongly about how she hoped that they would get a real shot at the American dream.

Patsy's apartment was on the small side but exquisitely decorated. I tremendously enjoyed sitting there and talking with her. One evening, I opened up to her about my Mennonite background and my decision to go against my family's wishes and make myself available for the draft during the Vietnam War. Over the years, through the things she said, I realized that this made a tremendous impression on her. During the last Fourth of July that she was to spend on this earth, one of the final, fully coherent sentences she would say to her nurse was, "You know, my husband was in the military."

In November of 1976, an unusual incident jolted us both and made us realize just how much we cared for each other. On the evening of November 14, I was returning from a business trip to Denver. The Texas International Airlines DC-9 was in full throttle for takeoff and had just barely lifted off the runway when the pilot, without warning, cut the engines and put them in full reverse. We were already near the end of the runway, so the plane came back down and went careening out across a field. Everyone had automatically assumed the "emergency crouch" position, and we did not know what to think. The landing gear had collapsed, and the plane was bumping wildly. After what seemed like ages but was probably only a minute or so, I looked up and saw nothing but flames outside the windows on both sides.

The plane finally came to a rest, leaning on the left side. I was seated on the right side by the emergency exit with a Shell geologist I had known from a previous meeting. We opened the emergency door and proceeded to jump off the wing, avoiding the flames, to the ground. One lady who jumped broke her ankle, so we carried her to a gathering spot about a hundred yards from the plane. Upon arrival at the gathering area, we discovered that the pilots had been the first to get out. So much for going down with the ship! We stood there in the dark and watched the plane completely burn up, but it did not explode. The pilots had aborted the flight because they had received a stall warning (later determined to be false) and they did not want to have to proceed out over the Rocky Mountain Arsenal, a chemical plant, which was in the flight path, for fear of having to crash land there.

You can imagine Patsy's surprise when I called to tell her this experience.

Besides our long talks, we enjoyed many other activities together: jogging in Memorial Park; rugby games where I played and Patsy watched; and during the winter of 1976, a ski vacation to Colorado. One of the most memorable trips, however, was to visit Patsy's family in Little Rock, Arkansas, for Christmas 1976. Patsy's siblings and parents were all there, and it was such a grand time. We ate and drank into the late evening sharing stories and talking about the past year.

Suddenly, Patsy rushed in and said, "Heidi's sick. We'll have to take her to the vet." A few of us hustled down the road to the veterinarian to determine why Heidi, the Mayer's pet schnauzer, was seemingly unresponsive. Only a few minutes passed before the veterinarian returned from his examination to give the prognosis. Heidi was drunk! Apparently, she had made herself right at home with many of the drink glasses sitting about the house. The Mayer family certainly celebrated Christmas in a manner the Lehmans would have not been able to imagine!

*****

The Lancaster County culture in which I grew up focused on the basics: hard work, honesty, and fairness. It often lacked a grand vision and was perhaps a bit naïve. I guilelessly took this training with me; and when Exxon offered me a spot at their research lab on Buffalo Speedway in Houston, Texas, I jumped. Research, such an idealistic vision! I quickly determined that, rather than being the highly vaunted "brains" of the organization, it was a backwater trap. The pace was agonizingly slow, and I quickly determined that the real work and focus of the organization was in operations. Within a few months of arriving at Buffalo Speedway, I began pleading with my bosses to get me into operations. Finally, in the fall of 1977, I was offered my choice of an operations job in London or New Orleans.

For Patsy and me, this was a catalyst in our relationship. Unfortunately, my earlier relationship was still baggage I had yet to unpack. It left me unable to think or feel freely about the choice at hand. Frankly, I was just plain scared. I felt that I did not fully understand what shortcomings of mine had torpedoed that marriage. But I knew, because of the beliefs Roy and Esther had bestowed in me, a repeat of that would likely doom me emotionally for a long time, perhaps forever. We discussed the situation at length, with me feebly trying to get my points across. I suggested that, as a way to decrease the risk, perhaps we should just move in together and postpone discussion of marriage for another day. I will never forget the blustery fall day I was in her apartment; and she said to me—in what must have been an act of courage for her—"Either marry me or adios." Then rather than recognizing how emotional this was for her as well and maintaining a dialogue, I did one of the dumbest, most short-sighted, most regrettable things I have ever done. I headed off to New Orleans by myself.

In New Orleans, I enthusiastically dove into my longed for operations job with Exxon. I began to date other girls, explore the city, and generally act like a bachelor. It was not as satisfying as I hoped, and I began to sense that my personal life was going in a circle.

In the spring of 1978, longtime friends of Patsy's, Sally and Hugh Burnett of Little Rock, Arkansas, were in Houston. Sally and Patsy visited at length, and apparently, the topic of discussion was how badly this guy in New Orleans had done her in! Sally, in a brilliant bit of intuitiveness, discussed the matter with Hugh. They decided that, rather than drive straight back to Little Rock, they would divert to New Orleans and take Patsy with them. Patsy called me up to ask about coming over on a certain date. I was equally surprised, thrilled, and apprehensive upon getting the call.

When Patsy arrived to spend the weekend, our time apart had shown me clearly, brilliantly, that one thing was for sure: I never would find someone as beautiful, sharp, and witty as Patsy. I knew that I could grow into a loving relationship over time with her. I believe that she had also come to perhaps appreciate some of my apprehension. We talked to each other for hours. Rather than just act scared, I bared my soul. I told her how devastating it would be for me if I got into another marriage that went sour. I told her how concerned I was that my career with Exxon would likely mean at least a few moves, and while she had moved out of Little Rock to Houston, in Houston she had lived in the same apartment for over ten years! We talked and talked and beginning that weekend began to rekindle and repair our relationship. Over the next few months, we regained the fun spirit we had previously had together.

I was still, if not scared, at least more than a little concerned about what I was getting myself into. However, as much as my earlier mistake had devastated me, I began to gain one key insight, which was confirmed over the years. Whatever other factors may have gone into that first failed relationship, the most important issue was that she had not really wanted to get married in the first place. "If there ten are reasons, and one of them is that you didn't want to be there in the first place, the other nine don't matter."

I sensed that Patsy not only wanted to get married but also wanted to get married to me. A simple concept, but the Dutchman was a slow learner on some scores! Patsy would frequently come to New Orleans, or I would go to Houston for the weekend. Early in the summer, Patsy invited me to go on a camping and canoeing trip on the White River in Northern Arkansas. I had never really explored Arkansas outside of Little Rock, and on this trip, I realized that some of Arkansas could be really out in the sticks in a way that Lancaster County couldn't match. As we headed to the spot where we were going to put our canoe into the White River, we realized that we had forgotten to buy any beer, wine, or other such beverages. I stopped at a grocery store and, not seeing any such things for sale, inquired into where one could buy some beer. "I'm sorry, but this is a dry county, no alcohol for sale." However, after a brief pause, during which he probably figured I wasn't a cop, he continued, "Mister, go east on this road for about two miles. On the right, there will be a concrete block building. Stop there, and you will be able to buy what you're looking for."

We proceeded down the road the prescribed distance and came to a fifty-by-fifty-foot concrete block building, with no windows and only one door. Inside, I saw that the checkout counter, rather than being by the entry door, was in the center of the room. There was no handle on the inside of the door; a pulley-and-rope system allowed the person manning the checkout counter to open the door so that you could leave when he thought so and not otherwise. Seeing my amazement, the clerk proceeded to further show me the .30-caliber rifle he had under the counter and explained that, this being a dry county, if any law officers were to come in and try to enforce that he would have them at his mercy. I decided that it would not be prudent to ask too many more questions, so I quickly made my purchases and got out of there. After he pulled on the rope!

Patsy had borrowed her dad's canoe and camping gear. Once we got onto the river, we had a great couple of days: very secluded but beautiful and with an intense quiet that was tremendously relaxing. On one occasion, the water became a bit turbulent as we went over a small rapid. Patsy became concerned that we were going to upset the canoe and ruin, or lose, all of her dad's camping gear. At this time, I declared in a voice of supreme confidence, "Patsy, we just need to keep paddling. This canoe is not going to upset." "This canoe is not going to upset" became our battle cry over the years whenever we got ourselves into a sticky situation.

*****

In early 1978, Patsy's family was given the bad news that Teddy had colon cancer. As the only unmarried sibling, and the oldest daughter, Patsy began spending time in Little Rock visiting with her dad and helping Robbie take care of things. Teddy underwent several operations, but his prognosis worsened throughout the year. By early summer, it became apparent that Teddy's health was failing rapidly. Patsy and I had more than moved past where we had previously broken things off, and I was beginning to see that, scary as it might be, I would likely never again get the opportunity to have someone in my life that was so perfect for me. Beautiful, caring, sharp, strong, and self-confident enough to be able to handle the Dutchman quite nicely, thank you.

I also began to sense something else. Patsy and her dad were very close, and his illness was devastating to her. I knew that it would mean the world to her if we could get married while her dad was there to walk her down the aisle.

Patsy and I were married on September 2, 1978, in Trinity Episcopal Cathedral in downtown Little Rock, Arkansas. It was a small, mostly family affair, but all of our close relatives were in attendance. The wedding picture I remember most vividly was Patsy in her beautiful flowing white dress with a beaming Teddy in his tuxedo next to her. It was a happy day for us all.

Teddy would pass away within six months of the wedding.

PART 3

Family and Friends

6

Willow Street

"Patsy, please be careful. What are you doing up on that stepladder?"

The small shotgun single on Willow Street in New Orleans had seemed the smart choice when we bought it. In the early summer, when it looked like Patsy and I would be getting married, I began preparing. My first move was to drive to Little Rock to ask Teddy for his daughter's hand in marriage—very old school but important to me. I reflected a lot on my upbringing during this period. Growing up Mennonite paved a path that was often hard to stray from. Their guiding tenants permeated the community and the family, holding us together, sometimes mulishly so. The war had started me on a separate path years before, but the hard work and honesty I had learned since I was boy had helped me forge my way confidently. Walking up to Teddy that night was nerve-racking. Past pains swirled around, but I stayed grounded in what I knew: that hard work, honesty, and mutual respect were going to make this marriage work.

I remember Teddy saying to me, "Well, just remember, Dave, if they don't have a little fire in them, it gets boring." His only words of wisdom were about Patsy's strong will! After asking her father, I felt that the next step was to have a house we could move into for the start of this next chapter. Patsy and I had discussed it some, but knowing Daisy Duck as I did it, I knew that we would be happiest if we could dive into the city and its treasures. This meant a house in, or close to, the Garden District. I found the best thing I could afford, bought it, and proposed to Patsy in front of it. I remember calling to talk to my dad afterward, a little nervous about what he was going to say. I knew it might not be much, but his responses were important to me. He said, "Well, that's good, Dave. If you live by yourself for too long, you get into the habit of living by yourself."

In New Orleans, "shotgun single" was used to describe a one-story house, very narrow in width but deep, with the rooms stacked from front to back. One could shoot a shotgun through the front door, and it would come out the back having gone through every room not hitting anything if the doors were all open. It was quaint-looking for sure, with two gaslights on the front porch, a large tree in the front yard, and a little white picket fence. As we moved our belongings into the house, it became apparent that our tiny new home lacked many of the accoutrements one gets accustomed to in newer houses; most striking was the complete lack of closets! Patsy immediately set her mind to making it as well decorated and furnished as her old apartment. This accounted for me frequently finding her on the top of a stepladder, paint roller in hand, a splatter or two across her front, adding a fresh coat of paint to the walls and ceilings. Many days she would still be in her nightgown, having gotten straight up out of bed to paint all day. Although the rooms were tiny, the ceilings were sixteen feet high. Patsy would be at the top of the ladder, undaunted in her zeal for a great-looking home. The high ceilings and nearly floor-to-ceiling windows presented a separate challenge for her. Patsy decided that we needed new drapes, well made, with top-quality fabric. But these types of drapes were not quite in the Lehman family budget. What to do? Well, Patsy bought the fabric, including the linings, and I bought a sewing machine! We worked together and made those drapes by hand. They looked great, I promise. But I know that there were many days when Patsy wondered what she had gotten herself into: she waited until her early thirties to get married, had dated astronauts and a future president of the United States, and here she was, practically a prairie woman having to paint and drape her own house!

On September 2, 1978, we married and committed to our adventures together. After the wedding in Little Rock, we spent a three-day "minihoneymoon" at the famous old Arlington Hotel in Hot Springs, Arkansas. Apparently, when Patsy's youngest sister Kathy married Hoyt Hayes years earlier, Patsy took several of the girls at the wedding to a pet shop and bought some mice—which they proceeded to put in the newlyweds car. Well, the Hayes decided that fair was fair and it was time for payback. We parked our car at the Arlington and didn't retrieve it until it was time to go home to New Orleans. When the valet brought our car, he said to me, "Mister, I think you have something wrong with your car." The four mice, which the Hayes (and still-unnamed others) had discretely put into our car had burrowed under the backseat carpets. Unfortunately for everyone, three days was just too long for the mice to last without food or water. We had to drive all the way back to New Orleans with our heads out the window! After a few months, I gave up on ever getting rid of the odor and traded that car in.

In the spring of 1979, we went on our real honeymoon: a week in the Bahamas. We had moved the wedding up to make sure that Teddy would be there; the speed of it all prevented us from moving our honeymoon with it. We rented a moped and went out of the main town to a "secluded" beach to go swimming. When we got back on the moped and started into town, Patsy, sitting behind me, said, "Where are my sunglasses?" I felt my pocket quickly and said, "Where is my wallet?" I stopped. We searched, but we'd been robbed! How naïve we were to think that the beach was secluded. Apparently, people were hiding in the woods waiting for just such unsuspecting tourists. It did not inspire confidence when the police arrived to interview us, and it looked to us like they were young enough to have recently graduated from the local grade school. Not surprisingly, our things were never found.

Hoping to put the incident behind us, we went to a casino with slot machines. I gave Patsy a quarter to put into one of the machines. She pondered that move a long time. To her, it was a huge deal to spend that quarter without the promise of getting anything back! It said a lot to me. I remembered when we first met and she showed me how she meticulously rationed her take-home pay as a teacher to afford nice clothes and travel. She was very proud to say she supported herself and these luxuries all on her own. You couldn't do that by throwing away quarters!

Our first few years together were quite an adventure. For one thing, there was the food: we loved going to Felix's Restaurant and Oyster Bar for oysters on the half shell. I had never had them before, but Patsy had learned to enjoy them with her dad. Then there was Mardi Gras. How would those folks back in Lancaster County react to folks drinking all day, riding around in garishly decorated floats, and throwing away beads? What a sight.

By far, the best thing that happened in New Orleans was the birth of our daughter Lisa. Before we got married, Patsy had explained to me that she suffered from an extreme case of endometriosis, a painful condition caused by growths on a woman's reproductive organs, and that we may not be able to have children. I was not dissuaded by this and knew I wanted her in my future even if our family could not grow. You can imagine our surprise when a few months after the honeymoon we found out that Patsy was pregnant. *Wow*, that was easy!

We got right into the swing of things with birthing classes and fixing up a nursery. On the morning of June 9, 1979, we went to the airport to pick up Patsy's mother, who was going to stay with us for a week or two to welcome the new baby. On the way back from the airport, Patsy began experiencing contractions, so we wheeled right off Interstate 10 to Lakeside Hospital, and within a few hours, we had our precious baby. We named her Mary Elizabeth Lehman. Mary was her mother's formal name; Elizabeth was my mother's middle name, and we nicknamed her Lisa.

This all came about so quickly that we decided to be a bit more careful for a while. This may have been a mistake. Later when we tried for number two, Patsy's condition had evidently advanced too far, and we were not successful. This ended up being one of our biggest regrets over the years.

We've always said, though, that if we could only have one child, Lisa was a perfect one. Patsy and I had so much fun with her as a baby in New Orleans. We had a bright red Silver Cross pram-style baby stroller nearly the size of a small car. She practically became a fixture riding on my shoulders. On one noteworthy occasion, we had arranged to sell one of our cars. Meeting in a store parking lot to conduct the transaction, I was preoccupied with counting the bills, and when it was all over, I suddenly thought, "Where's Lisa!" The moment I turned to move, I realized she was still on my shoulders!

Both Robbie and my parents came to visit us several times in New Orleans. On one occasion, I got the chance to show my dad around the office where I worked. I remember as he looked in amazement at a deep seismic line from the Gulf of Mexico. He was mesmerized by the technology, and one could almost see his mind working, wondering what might have transpired in his life if he had been afforded some different opportunities.

We have a picture from one of their visits, a favorite of mine. It's of my parents, taken from a side angle as they were sitting on a boat in the Mississippi River, with the city of New Orleans in the background. They look so solid, rugged, and steady compared with such a wild city—two Rocks of Gibraltar.

The Mennonite community had given my family foundations that set my siblings and me up for achievement. Our resiliency frequently gave way to success, but as I grew older, I wonder if it had done a disservice to our family as well. My parents were actually less structured than many in the community, but conformity and inflexibility had shaped their lives and contained them in ways a different community would not have. I always enjoyed when they came to visit me and held on to the gratitude I felt when they were around. I wished they could have experienced more and think about how they would react to the changes in the world today.

Glen Buck was a really nice guy, and that's about all I can say for him. The sixty-two-year-old geologist had been assigned to be my "mentor" on my first operations assignment in New Orleans. I liked him a lot, and we shared some good experiences, but as far as mentoring goes, I pretty much picked up what he knew in a week. I tried not to show my impatience, but I'm sure that it must have been apparent to him. The powers that be saw that I was ready to move on and transferred me to an offshore production assignment. Part of that assignment involved logging wells in the offshore Gulf of Mexico. Geologists log wells during the drilling of an oil or gas well. After the well is drilled, electrical and other measuring devices are lowered in on the end of a cable. The geologist commonly determines which instruments are to be put into the well and then is the first to see and interpret the readings that come through. The results are key in the decision on whether to "run pipe" in the well (i.e., whether to cement an expensive string of steel casing into the well in preparation for production or whether to plug it as a dry hole). This was a lot of responsibility for a young geologist, and I couldn't get enough.

The potentially exciting part involved getting to and from the shore to the rig or platform where the well was being drilled. The typical mode of transportation was by helicopter. When the winds were high, this could be somewhat dicey. I remember one particularly windy day when the helicopter pilot told me as we approached the rig, "I'm at the limits of control in this wind, so I'm going to touch down, but am not slowing down the rotors. You have five seconds to get off, and then I'm out of here."

When the winds were too high, I had to ride out to the rig in a workboat. These workboats were about 100 to 150 feet long and about 30 feet wide. They had a cabin up front and an open flat rear for transporting materials to the rigs. Once it arrived, the workboat would back up toward the rig, and a crane would lower hooks to pick up the materials. In the event a geologist or other person was on the boat, a "crew basket" was lowered. The crew basket was an open basket with a round bottom about eight feet in diameter and webbed netting about seven feet high all the way around. Since the reason for being on the workboat was strong winds, the seas were typically throwing up swells ten feet high or more.

Getting onto the crew basket could be a challenge to say the least. The crane operator would typically try to lower the crew basket so that it landed on the boat deck at the bottom of a large swell. The geologist would jump on the minute it hit the deck, and the crane operator would immediately lift it skyward to get out of the way of the boat rising on the next swell. If it happened at night, one had the experience of being lifted the equivalent height of a thirty-story building or more in the darkness with the wind howling and the sea below. Roller coasters have nothing on this!

I was learning a lot at my job, having fun exploring New Orleans with Patsy, and of course, loving Lisa's arrival on the scene. But I was getting increasingly frustrated at work as we went into 1980 and 1981. The work could be interesting, but the stifling bureaucracy of Exxon was new to me and hard to handle. For example, one of my bosses decided that all geologists should have a drafting table in their office. My office barely had the space for me to sit at my desk, let alone more furniture. I decided that the drafting table was not needed and single-handedly moved it to a storeroom down the hall. This caused a huge stir, and looking back, I'm surprised he did not just fire me!

It was during this time in New Orleans that I formulated a strategy for my career, which pretty much guided how we lived for the next twenty-five years. There are several decisions I made that I have debated with myself and frequently with Patsy ever since. Following the Arab oil embargo of 1973, the price of oil had risen dramatically, and as a result, the late 1970s and early 1980s were a boom time for the oil business. Many geologists were recruited heavily by headhunters and would leave for salaries exorbitantly higher than what they were being paid at Exxon.

In 1980, Patsy and I took a trip to Houston and were invited to a party at Jim Glanville's house. Patsy and Jim's wife Jill were second cousins, and we were also close friends. During the party, Jim and two friends of his, whom I'll just call Bert G. and John S., took me aside to have a talk. Jim was in the commercial real estate business, Bert was an engineer who had started his own oil company, and John had started his own bank catering to the oil industry. The gist of their message to me was that business in Houston was great. Opportunities to make a fortune were there for the taking—all I had to do was get on with it and ditch Exxon!

Although I had already demonstrated a willingness to part with established ways and do things differently, I was actually quite reluctant. Over the years, I had observed several things about the oil business that made me think twice. First of all, I was doing pretty well with Exxon. It was the premier oil company, and my superiors had assured me that I had the potential to achieve a very senior level if I stuck with it. Secondly, although I liked the idea of being in a smaller company or even my own company, my upbringing had not given me a good business background, and I felt that I had more to learn. Whether this was more a lack of confidence or knowledge, I don't really know. But I knew that the oil business, while it allowed for significant financial rewards, could also be a tough business.

I watched geologists, engineers, landmen, and others switch companies for a large increase in salary and then get laid off shortly thereafter when a particular play or geologic idea went bust. Through all of this, I decided that I would stick with Exxon as long as my career was progressing and that when I left, I would work for myself, no one else. I suppose this was partly a result of my Pennsylvania Dutch upbringing—I didn't like to quit. In the back of my mind, I saw my Exxon career as an opportunity that I should not take lightly. I wanted to see how far I could ride that horse and keep providing Patsy and Lisa with as good a life as possible.

What really drove home the realities of the oil business for me was watching the fate of these three men. One went to jail, one went bankrupt, and one lost their house.

I ended up staying with Exxon for twenty-two more years. This involved eight more moves around the world and experiences I could have never imagined. Years later, after I left Exxon and enjoyed life much more, Patsy and I would debate the continued decisions I made to stay. I would say I should have left sooner, but to my surprise, she would generally take the position that the financial cushion I built during those years at Exxon had allowed me to do things I would not have been able to do otherwise. What a trooper!

In 1981, I got a promotion, and we transferred to Houston. Patsy could finally afford to hire a decorator, and no one had to make any drapes!

7

The Bayou City

Patsy may have escaped the rigors of making her own curtains, but she did not escape the Dutchman's propensity for doing hard work to avoid paying an extra nickel. We bought a nice house in a neighborhood considered far north of downtown Houston proper in 1981. It was north of FM (Farm to Market) Road 1960, and the growth of Houston had not moved that far north. It was a newly developed neighborhood, and we purchased a brick four-bedroom house on a modest-sized lot—a far cry from the shotgun single of New Orleans. However, we went from the vast culinary delights of central New Orleans to a paucity of taste in the immediate vicinity. Fortunately, we found a delicious barbecue place called Strack Farm Bar-B-Que, where Patsy and I developed our lifelong love of delicious Texas barbecue.

Having finished the usual undertaking of moving everything in, decorating, and making ourselves comfortable, we decided that a sprinkler system was needed. I decided I could do this myself—I was practically a certified ditch digger after Vietnam—but Patsy was right out there with me every step of the way, digging ditches and helping put a line underneath the driveway by "jetting" a hole with a garden hose. We spent hours digging long ditches and shoveling mounds of topsoil and compost to make lovely flowerbeds, but the crowning achievement of all our efforts was the mailbox. The developer installed a plain standard mailbox on a steel post. Most of our neighbors had handsome brick structures housing their mailboxes, so I decided to dust off my bricklaying skills learned back in Lancaster to build our own. We had fun with the project and put a time capsule filled with memorabilia of the time inside the structure. Thirty-seven years have passed, and I wonder how the time capsule is doing in there. I think it would be fun to drive by the place and "accidentally" run into the mailbox to open it up again.

About a block down the street, one of the neighbors was similarly preoccupied with working in his yard, shoveling large mounds of mulch and so forth. I joked with Patsy one day and told her, "I'll bet he's from Pennsylvania." We asked him one day as we drove by, and sure enough, he was.

Although we were living comfortably, I was cognizant of the fact that the house had been at the upper end of our "affordability" range, and we had bitten off a hefty mortgage. We were in the Carter era, so inflation was high, and the mortgage rate on the house was over 15 percent. I remember the incredulity on a coworker's face as I explained that it was not so bad because it was tax deductible! At any rate, we were watching our pennies pretty closely. In later years, Patsy would tell friends the story of how I had made her take a bag of groceries back to the store because I felt that we could not afford them. I honestly do not remember the incident—I know, how convenient—but I also know that the Dutchman could have pulled just such a thing.

At one point, Patsy had discovered a new trinket, which made a great back scratcher. She wanted to ease some of the financial burden and proposed that she go door-to-door selling them so that she could have enough money to buy me a Christmas present with her own money. I tried to explain that our money was always her money. Besides, I did not need much for Christmas and reminded her of the orange I received back at the Buck when I was a kid.

Despite removing that drafting table in New Orleans, I had landed a job as exploration supervisor in North Alaska for Exxon. It was a challenging new assignment for me and captured my attention. It involved regular travel to Alaska with a chance to see vast parts of that beautiful state and take part in the adventures it had to offer. My favorite Alaska story is a rather odd little tale. Exxon always did, still does, and will continue to do things thoroughly. Exxon arranged a ten-day trip for myself and other first-time supervisors to various parts of their Alaska operations. A Twin Otter, a two-engine turbo prop with room for maybe fifteen passengers, chauffeured a dozen of us around the state.

Starting from Anchorage, we went south to the pipeline at Valdez. This was before the big spill, so notoriety had yet to yank the covers back on this sleepy little port. From there, we flew north along the pipeline toward the production operations center at Prudhoe Bay and spent a night in Fairbanks along the way. Leaving Fairbanks, we took a side excursion east to the tiny old gold mining town of Fort

Yukon, aptly named as it sits right on the Yukon River. After landing on a dirt airstrip in the forest, we walked a few hundred yards through the woods and came to a clearing along the river with what looked like the remnants of an old Western: wooden buildings with most of the paint long since peeled off, dirt streets, and no people in sight.

We stopped in the largest building labeled Restaurant and Bar with the intent to get a cup of coffee. It was about ten in the morning. There were several older ladies sitting at a corner table drinking coffee and deeply engrossed in their conversation. Trying to be friendly, I walked over to them and tried to strike up a conversation. I said, "Ladies, this is a nice little town you have here. Now tell me, when you buy groceries, do you have to drive into Fairbanks?" One of the ladies looked up at me and said, "Sonny, if there was a road to Fairbanks, we wouldn't be here!" That's the way it is in much of Alaska.

My job continued to be interesting for me, and I performed well in my new role. One day, my manager referred back to my rough start in New Orleans and several other things I was unsure about at the time. He told me, "Dave, I've never seen anyone who could fall into a pile of sh*t and come out smelling like a rose as you." I'm not quite sure if it was meant as a compliment, but I took it as one.

After about two years in the job, I was approached about moving to Kingsville, Texas, and becoming the district production geologist, a great step forward for someone of my age and experience. Before leaving New Orleans, I had been offered an entry-level geologist job in Kingsville and turned it down. I did not think the job was going to challenge me, and I knew that Patsy would not like living in Kingsville, a small, slow South Texas town most noted for being at the edge of the King Ranch. People around the company joked, "It was not the end of the world, but you could see the end of the world from there." Now I was being offered the top job there for a geologist. My boss put it to me this way: "Anybody who is anybody in Exxon has been to Kingsville, so if you want to be somebody, you better get on down there too."

By this time, I was really beginning to like the oil-and-gas business, and turning down this job would be career ending as far as Exxon was concerned. I weighed my options, but I did not have enough of a financial cushion to form my own company, and most of the people I knew who took jobs outside of Exxon rarely ended up better off. Besides, I knew that this experience would put me in a much better position either within Exxon or for pursuing those options later on if I wanted. I presented all of this to Patsy, knowing that she would not like the prospect of two years at the end of the earth. She was a good sport about it but would tell friends that Route 59 should have been repaved after the heel marks she left when I dragged her the whole way down to Kingsville!

8

To the Edge

Turning south out of Houston on Interstate 59, heading toward Kingsville, Texas, and going through many of what my father used to call spaghetti bowl intersections, the overarching sensation is the flatness of the terrain. It's hypnotic. As you continue farther south, the city of Corpus Christi provides a small respite from the monotony as its skyline appears to the southeast. The landscape continues its unending flatness with hayfields giving way to cotton fields and cotton fields giving way to grasslands. The open grasslands contain cattle, although generally not the stout Angus and Hereford of the upper coast. Here are the famous Longhorns, known for their ability to withstand drier conditions. South of Corpus Christi the Santa Gertrudis show up. These stout red-colored cattle can also withstand dry conditions but yield significantly more meat than the lean Longhorns. They are bred from a mixture of Spanish and American cattle and were patented by the famous King Ranch. The sight of large John Deere tractors working this land reminded me of home— although some of them were so large they would have had a hard time turning around on the 120 acres at the Buck.

Three and a half hours south of Houston, Kingsville finally appeared on the horizon to the right. It definitely felt like I would be able to see the end of the earth from there.

In 1983, Kingsville was a town of about twenty thousand people and known for the following: the nearby headquarters of the King Ranch, a naval air training station, Texas A and I University (now Texas A and M University, Kingsville), a large petrochemical plant about five miles away, and the headquarters for Exxon's south Texas operations. The town was laid out in a grid, and the two-story Exxon building was the tallest in town. It was tan brick, blending right in with the dust, dry grass, mesquite trees, and Spanish architecture throughout the town.

There was a grocery store and several small restaurants, but you had to drive to Corpus Christi if you were looking for a clothing or department store. All the restaurants were "Tex-Mex," although occasionally one of the locals would try their hand at Italian, but it generally did not last long.

Our first night there, we stayed in a Holiday Inn by the high-way. I thought it would be the best option, but the roach that scurried across out hotel floor quickly dissuaded me of that thought. Patsy was mortified—she had left Little Rock for the big city and wasn't quite sure what she had gotten herself into here.

On an earlier scouting trip, I had located a small house for rent. My thought was that since this was a two-year assignment, we could persevere in a small place. It quickly became apparent that asking Patsy to move out of her custom-decorated house into this would be one sacrifice too many! About this time, a large home, swimming pool and all, came on the market in one of the best areas. The house had a heavy Spanish architectural influence and sat on a nice lot. We grabbed it.

Over the years, Patsy had always been my best financial and business advisor. This time was no different. We made a low offer on the house, which the owners accepted. However, when we went to close, we were informed that the lady had changed her mind and did not want to sell. I was nervous and knew that we would have trouble finding a good home on the prairie. However, Patsy was very calm and nonplussed. I can still see us sitting in our car discussing the matter when she simply said, "Don't worry. They will come around." Sure enough, within a day or two, they did.

Patsy and I, coming from religious backgrounds, and being religiously inclined ourselves, looked for a new church in Kingsville. Part of our reasoning was that we wanted to get Lisa christened on her sixth birthday. On taking a "prejoining" class at the Episcopal Church, it was explained that the three precepts of this church were scripture, tradition, and reason. This sounded right down my alley, and I agreed with Patsy that we should join. Aiding the decision was the fact that the reverend was a retired navy admiral.

On Easter Sunday, 1984, we held Lisa's christening, which was followed by a grand party at our house. Patsy put out her best silver, and we all pretended that we were right in the most elegant place in New Orleans. Among the guests were our friends (and cousins), Jim and Jill Glanville who had come down with their family from Houston for the event. We named Jim and Jill to be Lisa's godparents.

Our Sunday routine developed into a morning spent going to church followed by a Sunday drive. This drive was typically out to the King Ranch Headquarters area where we enjoyed seeing the majestic herds of Santa Gertrudis cattle and the ranch pastures. There was always this air of otherworldliness to it all.

For special occasions, or sometimes just for a change on the weekends, we would go to the King's Inn. It was this magnificent white wooden structure right on the water about a half-hour drive down the coast toward Brownsville. They specialized in a wide assortment of fresh seafood, much of it fried, and it was terrific.

The reason for our tour of the Texas prairie was Exxon's large presence there. Exxon had oil-and-gas leases on five large ranches, totaling more than five million acres. Even with Exxon's large presence in Prudhoe Bay, the North Sea, and other large oil fields around the world, this represented one of Exxon's most prolific drilling and production operations. The work was frenetic. We had almost twenty rigs running continuously; and the sixty or so geologists whom I supervised had the job of finding profitable drilling sites, logging the wells, and determining whether to set pipe. I would get calls at all hours from geologists wanting to confirm a pipe-setting decision. Although we were an important operation, the location was isolated, and local management had unusual authority for an Exxon operation. I loved all of it.

Despite the "everybody who is anybody at Exxon" talk that I had received before moving, in 1985, Exxon management determined that production in south Texas was peaking and new technology would allow for operations management without so many local offices. For perspective, when I first arrived in south Texas, there was not a computer in sight, and we managed a $100 million plus budget with handwritten spreadsheets. The Kingsville office was getting shut down, and operations would be moved to Corpus Christi. Although the half-hour commute was not that long, management deemed that all employees would move to Corpus Christi because of the intensive nature of the business. We would be moving again. Patsy was not happy about this but was ready to get to a more civilized location. We settled into a nice, albeit smaller, house on the western outskirts of Corpus Christi. She once again had to start over to decorate to her standards and accomplished it with her usual skill and aplomb.

This period was a difficult one for us as a couple. Although Patsy told me about her endometriosis before we were married, I knew I wanted to marry her regardless. If we were going to be each other's only family, that was still plenty for me. However, now that we had Lisa and enjoyed her so much, we both desperately wanted more children. While in Kingsville, we had consulted specialists, and both underwent a series of tests to see if we might overcome this. For Patsy, some of these tests involved trips to Houston, which she took by herself because I was "too busy." I have regretted that I did not take off to accompany her; and certainly later in life, I saw the error of my ways, becoming a much more attentive husband over the years. It did not happen overnight, as the farm boy is a slow learner. Despite our efforts, it was becoming slowly evident that our effort for more children was not going to succeed. We both quietly mourned for several years, not talking about it much. Patsy certainly would have been willing to, and I wish I had.

As another sign that our good fortune was just not clicking in Corpus Christi was when our first dog, Buffy 1, got off his leash and was hit and killed by a school bus as Lisa and Patsy stood waiting one morning. Already we were in a strange land and overwhelmed with everything else going on, this event certainly heightened the anxiety in the Lehman household.

A little while after all that, Patsy complained about what she thought was a large rodent lurking around the house. One Saturday, I sighted it on the back patio. I thought that I knew just the right antidote. I grabbed a 410 shotgun (a small-gauge shotgun) I had at the time, slid open the sliding door from the living room, and shot that rodent. It exploded everywhere. Blood, guts, and fur pasted the side of the house. Patsy was furious, and I thought I might be next!

In 1986, during our year in Corpus Christi, a seismic (no pun intended) event shook the oil-and-gas industry. High prices following the Arab oil embargo of 1973 had driven a huge expansion of the industry, and the resulting glut had led to an oversupply. In 1986, the chickens came home to roost, and a collapse in oil prices from

$40 a barrel to around $15 ensued. All the Exxon rigs in south Texas were immediately shut down. This is the type of event that led to the collapse of many businesses, of which mine might have been had I made a different decision in 1983.

The industry was still greatly affected, and Exxon informed me that due to the lack of drilling activity in south Texas, it was their intention to do away with my position. They were going to relocate us back to Houston, where I would be technical manager in the East Texas Production Division. This was quite a step-up and would involve me managing about one hundred geologists and engineers. It was also one of the few occasions in the company in which a geologist was assigned to supervise engineers. It was an innovative step and got quite a few folks' attention, especially the engineers!

Some of our friends and relatives—especially relatives—had a difficult time understanding the basis for all of our physical moves. We had some next-door neighbors, Jennifer and Frank, who were also friends of ours in Corpus Christi. When Patsy informed them that we were moving to Houston, Jennifer proclaimed, "Well, I just do not see why you let him jerk you around like that. I would not stand for it." A few weeks later, Frank told me that he and two of his colleagues at Forest Oil had been given the news from their manager that the Corpus Christi office was being shut down. They had the option of taking a job with Forest in Midland or leaving the company. They all said, "Well, let us go home, and discuss it with our wives." As they convened in the hallway afterward, they looked at each other and said, "What the hell are we thinking? The industry is in a complete slump. We either move or starve!" They immediately went back into the manager's office and informed him that they would all take the jobs in Midland. It was with a chagrinned expression that Jennifer informed Patsy that she was being jerked around as well!

It was not just the oil-and-gas producers and explorers like Exxon who were being impacted by this crash. One of the experiences I remember involved Tom, a vice president of Schlumberger. When things were booming and we had upward of twenty rigs running, we would let the geologists call up whichever oilfield services company they wanted to log the wells. Seventy per cent of the time, they called Schlumberger, or Big Blue as they liked to say. When times got tough, we insisted that the logging jobs be bid out. Schlumberger refused to bid—it was beneath them. Their percent of our business went from seventy to zero, so Tom was sent down from New York to get this straightened out. He hosted a lavish dinner on a riverboat in the middle of Corpus Christi Bay. I sat directly opposite him at the middle of a long table. About midmeal, he started in with the Schlumberger pitch. I said, "What you are telling me is that Schlumberger is the Cadillac of the business." He pounded the table and said, "Absolutely!" I had to inform him that we did not really need a Cadillac and, with times being tough, we could get by with an old Ford pickup.

In 1986, we moved to Kingwood, Texas. It is a "master planned community" carved out of the pristine pine forests about twenty miles northeast of downtown Houston. Everything was laid out ahead of time, including the schools, community centers, and walking path—even the strips of the forest left behind were planned to give the area a woodsy feel. We found a brick two-story house with a swimming pool and backed up to a hiking trail. It was a short walk to school for Lisa, where she entered the second grade. Lisa swam for a local club called the Sand Creek Sea Lions. Patsy loved the neighborhood feel and became very active in the local garden club. We made lifelong friends here, including Debbe and Edward Chin. Years later, one of our last trips together would be to their son's wedding in New York City.

Lisa's second-grade teacher, Mrs. Lossman, and her husband also became friends of ours. She was an excellent teacher and pronounced Lisa to be one of her favorite pupils but counseled that Lisa had a tendency to perfectionism. Lisa was learning the art of overdoing good things from her mother and father! It was during this time that I noticed the effect the moves were having on Lisa. I had bought Lisa a trampoline, which she loved and would jump on for hours at a time. We first installed it in our backyard in Kingsville. When we moved to Corpus Christi, it went into the garage. After about six months, Lisa came to me and said, "Dad, let's put the trampoline up." Sure enough, after about six months in Kingwood, she said, "Dad, let's put the trampoline up." Lisa was a bit of a shy kid, so it took a bit to adjust to the new setting. The frequent moves around this time were definitely an added stressor, but she was resilient. Each time we moved, it took about six months for her to mourn the old and come out swinging for the new.

My new job, as technical manager of the East Texas Production Division, proved to be an interesting challenge. This was my first time working with Rex Tillerson, who would later go on to become chairman of Exxon and then secretary of state. I supervised the geologists and engineers, and Rex was my counterpart as operations manager, supervising the field superintendents and pumpers. There was an intentionally built-in friction between the two positions. The geologists and engineers would frequently suggest work the field people thought was ridiculous, and then Rex and I would have to iron it out. We butted heads a lot, but Rex and his wife, Renda, eventually became good friends with Patsy and me. I later told him that if I had known that he was going to get to be chairman I would have treated him a lot nicer back in those East Texas days!

There is another incident I remember with Rex, now very amusing in hindsight. It was about 1988, and the Internet was being born. Exxon did not allow our computers to be connected to the outside world; but the Exxon technology folks, recognizing the potential of the tool, implemented something called the intranet, which was only for Exxon internal communications. They sent around a memo on this new technology. Upon receiving the memo, Rex came by my office to pronounce what he thought about it: "I don't know why they are wasting money on this. If I want to get a hold of someone, I just pick up my phone and call them!"

Exxon soon came up with a new position involving supervising international exploration activities with a focus on Southeast Asia. The oil-and-gas business is a worldwide business, and I thought this new position would give me a good overview of that. The added benefit was that it would give me a very visible position in the Exxon Exploration Company after having been lost for many years in the production side. Perhaps I might become president after all! The downside—it would involve a move to New Jersey, Yankee land.

Exxon culture was very insular and discouraged a lot of interaction with the outside world. The people we worked with tended to be the people we also spent our time with outside of the office. When Exxon moved all of us, it was easier to keep hanging out with the people we already knew rather than reach out to a new community. It was during this time that I realized some of the struggles Patsy was dealing with in our social circles.

Through all of the years we spent together, Patsy's sense of style never dulled, and my job allowed her to keep an even sharper closet, though those maroon leather pants from our early Houston days put up a good fight. The other Exxon wives didn't derive the same kind of pleasure from shopping as Patsy did and kept themselves rather plain. It sometimes created a friction within the groups that we never really discussed but that I wish I had tried harder to fix. Fortunately, the move to Jersey helped soothe this, although it presented other challenges.

9

Yankee Land

We moved to Montville, New Jersey, just across the river from New York in 1989. There is no better illustration of the cultural differences we faced in New Jersey than our housewarming party. In our previous neighborhoods, Patsy had always been welcomed with small gifts of food and overtly extended hands of friendship from the neighbors. She had reciprocated with welcoming parties for new neighbors and so forth. In New Jersey? Nothing. The attitude, although unspoken, seemed to be "What are you doing here, you were not born here, your parents are not from here—why are you here?" It did not help that the winters were long, and I was commonly away for weeks at a time on my new job. Lisa also had to learn to contend with a whole different situation in the school district. It was topped off one day when she came home with dirt and grease in her hair from being bullied by some of the other students. Patsy was at her wits' end and feeling lonely. Finally, she decided that she would rectify the situation by giving herself her own welcoming party. So she did the baking and invited the neighbors. They came, were very friendly, and by all accounts enjoyed themselves, though I doubt that the next new neighbor will get much different treatment than we received. Traditions, good and bad, die hard.

Montville is a pretty town in its own right. Unlike Houston, the trees were mostly hardwoods and were beautiful when the leaves changed in the fall. In the winter, however, they were barren. Long nights and cold weather compounded the feeling of isolation. An unexpected and disorienting characteristic up here was the roads. The sprawling, flat expanse of Texas allowed for an organized system of community building. Our neighborhood in New Jersey was decidedly not this way. The age of the area, alongside the geography, contributed to its disorder. One could be going east one minute and, still on the same road, start heading west the next. One night, Patsy and I were trying to find a friend's house for dinner. Patsy was driving, and my navigation had gotten us totally lost. To fix the situation, I insisted she make an illegal U-turn. She got her first ever traffic ticket, and I stared studiously at the map as she glared at me all the way to our friend's house.

Fortunately, not everything was terrible in this part of the world. We were much closer to family. My dad had passed away when we were in Kingsville, but my mother still lived on the family farm, and we were able to visit her more regularly. My sister Margaret lived in Palmyra, and my brother Roy lived in Philadelphia, so we also saw them more often. My other brother, Tom, and his family came to see us one year as well. We took their boys, Kyle and JT, to the top of the Empire State Building when they were about nine and ten years old, and we still reminisce about that visit. Patsy's sister Kathy, her husband Hoyt, and their two boys came to visit. The boys loved New York but told me years afterward that the two things that impressed them were when I did a U-turn in my jeep by jumping the curb to correct my direction when I got lost and when I bribed a store clerk at Toys-R-Us to let them in after the store was past its closing time! I plead the fifth on that.

Every month or two, I would be off for a tour of Exxon's Exploration and Production activities in Southeast Asia: Australia, Indonesia, Malaysia, and Thailand. Other than my previous stint in Vietnam, which did not allow for much sightseeing, this was my first real tour of that part of the world. It was about thirty hours door to door to get over there, which made for some long stretches away from home. Patsy endured, even during the long winter nights in this far-off and sometimes unfriendly land.

The executive vice president of Exploration for Exxon had had his eye on me for a while and decided that I needed to "stamp my ticket" with a tour as assistant to the upstream director of Exxon in the headquarters staff. During this time, the Exxon headquarters were moving from downtown New York to Las Colinas, Texas, a northwestern suburb of Dallas. Another move.

10

To the Other Side
of the World

Patsy did not like moving, but she was happy to be getting back to Texas. We moved to Dallas in 1991. Unfortunately for Lisa, we had gotten her into the town's private school, but she was only able to spend a total of three months there before having to move on. When she had to explain this to her teachers, almost all of who had spent their entire lives in that part of New Jersey, they just could not understand.

My job in Dallas entailed keeping the upstream director appraised on what was happening in the exploration and production business around the world: reviewing and preparing projects to be approved by him or the Exxon board. It was a competitive posting, but for me, it meant being even further enmeshed in large company bureaucracy!

One of the perks of moving from New Jersey to Dallas was the drop in housing prices. We settled into a more spacious house with a huge kitchen that was perfect for Patsy. She loved to cook, and with all of the moves, dinner at the table helped ground the family and allowed us to adjust to our new environments together. I tried to make it home for dinner as often as possible and loved hearing about everyone's day, especially after all of the process-oriented meetings I spent my days in.

The move back to Dallas provided a morale boost for the whole family. Patsy was far more comfortable on this side of the Mason Dixon line, and Lisa loved her new school, the Hockaday School for girls. Our previous history in Texas also made this move seem like coming back, instead of starting over. I was able to reconnect with old friends, including Rex and an old friend from F&M, Bill Walker.

Indeed, one of the high points for me was the opportunity to reconnect with and get to know Bill a little better. Years earlier, when I had gotten disgruntled with my Exxon job in New Orleans, I had gone to talk to Bill in Dallas, and he had offered me a job as a geologist working for his family oil-and-gas company. I appreciated the offer but felt that the scope of opportunity doing that was beneath my ambition. Now that I was living in Dallas, Bill and I spoke by phone and had lunch on a regular basis. Patsy and I frequently joined Bill for dinner, and he and I had several memorable dove hunts in south Texas.

Rex and I overlapped for about a year in Dallas. I had the exploration side of the business, and Rex had the production side. Even though we butted heads, we had since grown enough in our roles that our competitiveness gave way to a comfortable friendship.

One morning, our boss, the upstream director for Exxon, abruptly called us into his office. We did not know what to expect, as getting a call like this was practically like being summoned by the Almighty. As it turned out, he wanted to inform us that his wife (of many years and six kids) had just served him with divorce papers. A colleague later told us that she had them served through a court official as he stepped onto the train to the airport for his weekly commute from his home in Toronto to Dallas. Apparently, when the headquarters moved to Dallas from New York, his wife came down for her first visit to Texas on a hot August day, got off the airplane, proclaimed that this was an oven, and promptly headed back northeast never to be seen in Texas again.

In my later years, I have regretted that Rex and I did not really talk about much besides business. Rex's wife, Renda, was a former cowgirl, and she and Patsy got along famously: they were vivacious, outgoing, loved to talk, and stood apart from many of the other wives at this time.

Although we had a comfortable life in Dallas, this was not going to last forever: these types of jobs were designed as two-year stints. My new position was to be exploration manager for Exxon in Malaysia. I had looked around and thought about it a lot but did not see any opportunities that would have been a better option. The career path at Exxon promised much more than almost any other company that interested me. Although Patsy did not relish moving, I also did not think that she would enjoy, nor would it be fair, to put her in a position where she might have to return bags of groceries to the store! The bust in 1986 had made me wary of moving to a company that could not withstand a market depression. We discussed it at length and decided that this opportunity would be the best option for us.

Patsy was particularly unexcited about this move, as she had travelled to Malaysia with me when we lived in New Jersey. Upon arriving at the airport in Kuala Lumpur, she experienced the "squats." They are holes used in lieu of a commode and are a mainstay of Southeast Asia. My Southern Belle wondered what she was thinking when she agreed to this.

The logistics of this move were far more complicated than any we had done before. First came the unpleasant task of informing Lisa, who at this time, in October 1993, was just beginning the ninth grade. We took her to a restaurant after church and informed her as we ate. She cried for hours. I could hardly stand it and truly questioned if I had made the right decision. Later, she begged us to stay at Hockaday on a boarding basis. Patsy and I looked back on this for a long time after wondering if we had made the right decision. We talked her out of it and made our decision final. We felt very strongly about the family staying together and knew she was going to a strong international school that we also felt would be an exciting life experience. As part of the bargain, she made me promise to book a vacation in Australia, which I delivered on. It took her about seven months to stop discussing the Hockaday option, which, while a bit longer than the trampoline, was a nice indication that she was settling into Malaysia.

The sense of "uprootedness" which came with having to go so far away drove many of our discussions when planning for the move. Patsy wanted to keep the house so we would have a home to return to, but the odds of us coming back to Dallas were slim. Even harder for Patsy was the car. Patsy had bought a maroon red diesel Mercedes about six years earlier when we were in Houston. She loved that car and the independence it gave her. Taking it to Malaysia was out of the question because they drive on the opposite side of the road in Malaysia. We looked into storage, but it just didn't make sense. Then there were the furniture and household goods. We would be allowed to take one large cargo container of goods with us. Everything in the house was marked "ship" or "store." It is a bittersweet experience to categorize the items of your life. On the day of the move, the movers took all of our objects into their proper "ship" or "store" contain- ers. Patsy watched as one of the "store"-labeled pieces was loaded, a kitchen hutch she had bought in New Orleans. She suddenly pro- claimed that she could not bear to part with that, and it was rerouted to the "ship" container. She was having a hard time getting used to this.

On the day in early December 1993 that we were to fly from Dallas to Kuala Lumpur, Patsy's two sisters and mother came to the airport to see us off. It was long enough ago that they actually came onto the plane with us. There was much storytelling, laughter, and even more so tears. This tight-knit group was seeing their own go-off- to-God-knows-where. The other side of the world might as well have been Mars as far as they were concerned. They were not sure they would ever see us again, but I knew that Patsy would never let all of those "store" containers sit unhoused for long.

11

Malaysia

Malaysia is a predominantly Muslim country, but that statement hides a rich mosaic of cultures and lifestyles. About 60 percent of the population is Bumiputra: people of the land or the native island population. They practice Islam. Thirty percent of the population is Chinese, and they are mostly Buddhist. Ten percent of the population is Indian and practice the Hindu faith. There are various denominations of Christians, but even all lumped together, they only constitute a small minority. The government has taken the innovative approach of declaring Islam as the official state religion while simultaneously proclaiming that there is freedom of religion in the country. This mixture of peoples works together well; they mostly keep to their own as far as socializing and celebrations of various life events. However, the three groups did not always coexist so peacefully. Malaysia was a British colony from 1867 until it gained its independence on August 31, 1957. In the early 1960s, without the British imposing rule, deadly riots broke out between various groups, primarily the Bumiputra and the Chinese. Mahathir Mohamad, the first prime minister of Malaysia, oversaw the institution of laws that basically mandated peace between the groups. The citizens were forbidden, under penalty of arrest, from saying anything negative in public against a different ethnic group. Regardless of what you think of the means, it stopped the spread of violence, forcing people to be civil until enough time went by that they began to, somewhat, accept each other's positions.

On a map, Malaysia looks like a type of broken *U* as it is made up of two parts. The first part, Peninsular Malaysia sits on a peninsula at the very end of a strip of land that snakes out from Thailand into the South China Sea. This section of Malaysia ends in a set of tiny pincers where Singapore sits. Across the sea from here is the island of Borneo. The northern third of Borneo contains the two Malaysian provinces of Sabah and Sarawak; the Sultanate of Brunei is nestled between the two.

Kuala Lumpur, the capital city of Malaysia, is an inland city located on the peninsula, about a third of the way north of Singapore. When I was there, it was a city of about a million people with an expat population of about a thousand. The city was sitting on the edge of the old and the new. Much of the population lived in small huts and open-air stalls lined many of the streets. On the other hand, modern shopping centers were being built, and new development was happening all around the city. Unlike many expat assignments where companies would build a self-contained compound for their employees so that they could enjoy the comforts of home and also be safe, in KL, we lived in homes, interspersed with natives and other expats throughout the nicer parts of the city. Our house was fairly large but a bit unconventional to say the least. The entrance was at the end of a long lane that wound between the lots on either side of us, so we were off the street a ways. Upon entering the house, one encountered a large fishpond built into the floor about four feet wide, thirty feet long, and three feet deep. Fish of all sizes filled the pool and made for quite a conversation piece with visitors. It was two stories with the main bedrooms upstairs and a smaller bedroom downstairs near the kitchen for the live-in housekeeper/cook. We had a television set. However, there were only three local stations, and they were all in Bahasa (the Malay language). Satellite TV had not yet made its debut, so we did not watch much TV.

The weather in Malaysia is also worth noting. Located essentially on the equator, it was hot and humid. There were two seasons—the rainy season and the dry season. During the dry season, it rained about three days a week, and during the rainy season, it rained every day. These were not like the daylong rains that are common on the Texas gulf coast. It would get cloudy around midafternoon, rain heavily for an hour or so, and then clear up.

The Lehman family arrived in Kuala Lumpur in December 1993. Lisa was in the middle of ninth grade—a tough period that the move was definitely not helping. While our house was being readied and we waited for the furniture to arrive, we lived in a high-rise apartment. Every day when I arrived home, Lisa and Patsy would be sitting around the kitchen table commiserating about their sad state of affairs and crying. It was a lot for me to bear. Christmas was coming, and all of our belongings were in a shipping container somewhere in the middle of the Pacific Ocean. Patsy decided that she would try to make the best of the situation, so she did some research and decided that, since we could not have a traditional Christmas, we would do something really unusual. She arranged a trip to northern Thailand, and we spent Christmas Day of 1993 riding elephants through the jungles of Thailand. In our little hotel, a piano player was doing his best rendition of Louis Armstrong's song "What a Wonderful World." In his accent, it came across as "I dink to myself, what a vunderful vurld." We nearly fell off our chairs laughing at the whole situation—with Patsy and Lisa laughing the loudest.

Nothing, and believe me nothing, can compensate a teenage girl for taking her out of her school and away from her friends in the middle of the ninth grade. Having said that, the International School of Kuala Lumpur (ISKL) was not a bad spot to land. It was funded by the large companies who had expats working in KL, and no expense was spared. Roughly half of the students were from Asia, including Japan, India, Australia, Indonesia, and local Malay students. The other half was European and American.

Lisa continued, as she had in the States, to be on the swim team and also played soccer. The ISKL teams competed against international and American schools throughout Southeast Asia; so when it was time for a swim meet or a soccer match, the students would fly to Singapore, Manila, Taipei, Jakarta, or Bangkok for their competition. Parents of the welcoming school usually housed the students, and they had some great experiences. We also enjoyed housing students from these other schools when they came to KL. Later, when Lisa went to college, she would tell me, "Dad, I don't even bother telling people what my high school was like. They think that I am making it up." We went to a few of her away meets but not most. Her first meet, in early January 1994, was in Singapore. When she got on the starting blocks, I saw some tears come to her eyes—this was so very different.

There were many interesting aspects to everyday life in KL, but none were more helpful or intriguing than Awah, the van lady. Awah was a Chinese woman who owned a medium sized truck outfitted with shelves and moveable sides. The truck was our local grocery store. Several times a week, Awah would pull into the driveway and prop up the sides of her truck, and the shopping would commence.

If she did not have something you needed, Awah would make sure to bring it back on the next rip. We loved her hard work, entrepreneurial spirit, and welcoming demeanor.

The golf test. This institution is one of the most unique traditions that I have ever witnessed. It was a huge deal among the expats in KL. While the British ruled Malaysia, they brought many things to the country so that their life there would resemble, as closely as possible, life back home in England. This included cricket pitches; racetracks; and, right in the middle of Kuala Lumpur, a proper golf course: Royal Selangor Golf Course.

Leisure time activities were limited in many respects here. TV was out. We were halfway around the world, so relatives could not readily come visit, nor could we easily visit them. There were no opera, football games, or anything like that. However, the Asians are crazy about golf. Many of the business activities were centered on golf matches. There were regular golf matches between Esso Malaysia and PETRONAS (our partner and the National Oil Company). I had often thought about taking up the sport but had never felt that I had the time. Patsy decided that if I was going to give it a try, she would also. When in Asia, do as the Asians do. So we prepared for the golf test.

One of the perks of being an Exxon executive in KL was a membership to the Royal Selangor Golf Club for both Patsy and me, with one catch. Although the company paid for the membership, the club was still run as an exclusive British-style club. While one might have been able to pay for a membership, in order to actually play on the course, one had to demonstrate "proficiency at golf." Each new member needed to play nine holes with a committee member. Committee members were local people who were basically on the board of the club. During the test, one had to demonstrate knowledge of the courtesies of golf (raking the bunkers, not stepping on the line of ones partner's putt, etc.) and shoot an acceptable score. This was deemed to be a forty-five for men and a fifty for women.

Now many of the expats taking this test were beginning golfers like Patsy and me. As you may or may not know, it is not easy (nearly impossible in fact) to pick up a golf club for the first time and shoot a forty-five or a fifty on nine holes. The expat community was very small in KL, so everyone knew when you were going for your golf test, and everyone knew whether you passed it or not; it was frequent topic of conversation. On top of this, there was an inherent unfairness in the way the executives and their wives were treated. It was widely known that, because of the perceived importance of the international businesses and their executives to the local community, the executives were rarely given a failing mark on the golf test, no matter how badly they played. However, their spouses were not accorded the same courtesy. Despite the fact that one was allowed to practice and retake the test as many times as necessary, there was a very strong sense of shame and ignominy associated with failing the golf test, especially among the women. Women were known to come home after failing the golf test and throw away their clubs never to pick them up again.

Patsy went to the driving range and began hitting balls. She found a local caddy, Sham, who, for a few dollars an hour, would spend hours with her. Sham would not only tee up the balls but would give her swing tips, from which she eventually developed a beautiful flowing swing that helped her win many a match back in the States. Patsy determined that she was not only going to take the golf test, but she was going to pass it on the first try.

My work in Kuala Lumpur was fascinating. All of Exxon's drilling was offshore in the Malaysian waters between Malaysia and

Vietnam. During my earlier trips to Malaysia from New Jersey, I had worked with local geologists to develop an exploration concept along the northern part of the offshore basin where Exxon had a concession, or land grant. Now that I was back and in charge of the operation, it was fun. There were sixty geologists and three supervisors in our group. There were a few expats; but the group was mainly Chinese, Indian, and Bumiputran. We made our first new oil field discovery with our exploration concept soon after I arrived in KL. Five more followed in the years I was there. Although this was a success in itself, I had my sights on another prize.

Historically, oil-and-gas drilling around Malaysia had been divided primarily between Exxon, offshore from the Malaysian peninsula, and Shell, which had the concessions offshore the eastern Malaysian provinces of Sabah and Sarawak. I thought there was more exploration potential around the eastern provinces and I was determined to go for it. One day, one of the supervisors reporting to me said, "Hey, Dave, a Shell geologist just gave a paper at a conference here, and I think that it shows how we might find some more oil fields in east Malaysia."

I listened to his ideas and thought that he had a point. From here it was a little tricky, because I had to convince Vishan, the exploration manager for PETRONAS, to award two large new offshore concessions directly to Exxon without going out to bid. I had been cultivating my relationship with him for years and was able to convince him that this was the right decision. Vu Cong was the exploration manager for Shell at this point. When he heard that I had taken two large exploration blocks right out from under him—and in Shell's traditional operating area no less—you could say he was less than pleased. Vu's father had been a senior official in the South Vietnamese regime and had arranged for Vu to get out of the country and go to school in the United States. In an interesting irony, when I was in Vietnam in 1969 and 1970, Vu Cong was earning a PhD in physics from the University of Pennsylvania.

The holiday celebrations were another interesting aspect of life in Malaysia. Muslim, Chinese, and Hindu holidays were all celebrated; but Christmas and Easter were not. Early on, Patsy and Lisa went to a Hindu ritual called Thaipusam. It is a celebration of Parvarti, the Hindu goddess of fertility and strength, and her son Murugan, the Hindu god of war. Parvarti gave Murugan a spear to vanquish the evil forces of the demon Surapadma. Participants in this festival put spears through their cheeks, pull loads up a hill with sharp hooks in their backs, and otherwise demonstrate seemingly impossible torture without bleeding or showing obvious signs of pain. The purpose of the festival is to pray to receive grace and destroy the bad traits within oneself. These cultural experiences never failed to expand our perspectives and instill a type of wonder that so many beliefs could coexist within the borders so peacefully.

Given that the majority of the population in Malaysia was Muslim, the dominant holiday was the monthlong Ramadan. It is a time of fasting and strict adherents do not eat or drink anything between sunup and sundown. It makes for some somber-looking people in the office, but one of the things that I noticed reminded me of growing up in Lancaster County: the tradition of the "hip pocket" Mennonite. This was the Mennonite farmer who was not supposed to drink but put a flask in his hip pocket so that he could have a swig or two while plowing the back forty, away from anyone's sight. Patsy's mother had later informed me that there was a strong tradition of "hip pocket" Baptists in the South. Well, while in Malaysia, we learned that there was an equally strong tradition of the "hip pocket" Muslim.

Chinese New Year was an especially grand and colorful event compared to the other holidays. It was typically a two-week celebration featuring parades, gaudy Chinese characters, and lots of multi-course Chinese meals. Chinese New Year was all the more noteworthy because the Chinese had a reputation of being extremely hard workers and many, especially in the construction and manufacturing industries, typically worked seven days a week, frequently without vacation, during the rest of the year.

Early in the history of the country, the tradition of the industrious Chinese led to enactment of legislation aimed at protecting the local Bumiputra population. Government agencies and companies with more than fifty employees had to have employee diversity that matched the ethnic mix of the population, i.e., it could not exceed 30 percent Chinese. Mahathir Mohamad, the first and long-serving prime minister, defended this controversial measure in a book entitled *The Malay Dilemma*.

In his book, Mahathir makes the argument that these islands belong to the Bumiputra people, whose ancestors have lived there for thousands of years and have passed them down. He writes about how the idyllic life on the island of fishing and collecting coconuts for food made the Bumiputra people soft. He believes that the Chinese are genetically superior because they have been suffering for thousands of years through wars, famines, and pestilence resulting in survival of only the fittest. Mahathir argues that because of this, if they allowed the natural course of things to take place, the Chinese would take those lands from the Bumiputra. He concluded such laws were necessary to hold onto what was rightfully the Bumiputra's.

Mahathir's argument is politically incorrect for those looking through its racial lens. However, he recognizes something that most who have been to the country would agree with: the voraciousness of the Chinese on the island would overrun the Bumiputra people if left unchecked. These laws serve to preserve a way of life. The local culture in Malaysia was quite laid-back, which made the contrast with the hard-working Chinese all the more apparent. For example, when a meeting was called for 8:00 a.m. in Malaysia, I would show up at 8:00 a.m. and typically be the first one there. For the meetings held in Singapore, where many of the managers were Chinese, showing up ten minutes early was still late. I would walk in, and there were no hellos or other introductions. It was simply, "Well, Dave's here. Now we can get started."

During our four years in Kuala Lumpur, we had several medical scares. During our first year there, Patsy went to the hospital with her first case of pneumonia. Evidently, the heat and humidity had taken its toll, and I later wondered whether this incident might have triggered a weakness in her lungs, which led to more medical complications later in her life. Fortunately, the doctors were able to get her back to good health, and it was an interesting contrast to the health scares we experienced with Lisa.

In May of 1996, I was on the east coast of Malaysia visiting some of Exxon's production facilities when I got a call from Patsy. Lisa was in the hospital with terrible headaches, but they couldn't figure out what was wrong with her. A heavy fog had set in, and flights back to Kuala Lumpur had been cancelled. In desperation, I commissioned a helicopter to make the two-hour flight across the mountains at nearly treetop level in the fog so that I could get back to the hospital in Kuala Lumpur. The hospital was an older facility in the center of the city. The paint was peeling, a layer of grime seemed to cover all of the surfaces, and an air of pain and desperation clung to you the moment you walked in. Lisa was curled up in pain on her bed, stuffed into a room with fifteen to twenty other patients. The doctors had no idea what was wrong and almost lazily diagnosed her symptoms as a migraine. Lisa had never had migraines before, and from what I knew of them, they didn't cause this type of reaction. After a day of watching Lisa suffer with no relief from her symptoms, I called around and, with the help of the Esso medical staff, located a modern facility in the suburbs of Kuala Lumpur. I remember hustling Lisa out of that old dilapidated place so fast we didn't even bother to check out. Patsy and I were in a full-blown panic by this time. At the newer hospital, they immediately took a spinal tap and determined that Lisa had viral spinal meningitis, thankfully far more treatable than the bacterial version. She was feeling better within a few days, and Patsy and I breathed easy again.

*****

As I sit here writing this on the Memorial Day weekend of 2018, one of the headlines in the international news is the large financial swindle perpetrated by the fund called 1Malaysia Development Bhd. This financial fraud occurred during Prime Minister Najib Razak's term and led to his overthrow in the latest election by none other than Mahathir Mohamad. Mahathir came back to save the country at the age of ninety-two! To those of us who lived there, it is not a surprise to hear of this fraudulent activity, as bribery and corruption are commonplace in many areas of the country.

A lighter example is the "thirty-five-ringgit traffic ticket." The locals told us that if a policeman stopped you for a traffic violation, you were to hand him thirty-five ringgit (the local currency, equal to about ten US dollars) along with your driver's license so you would not be given a ticket. I must somewhat sheepishly admit that I often wondered whether this was really true, and on one occasion, just to test it, I did in fact hand the officer the requisite thirty-five ring- git. It worked. One of my colleagues married a local woman named Sabrina and when it came time for them to move back to the United States, he felt compelled to sit down and tell her, "Now, Sabrina, if you get stopped in Texas for a traffic violation, *do not ever try to bribe a Texas state trooper.*"

*****

"Dad, let's go back to town. This is boring, and Mom and I are soaked in sweat."

It was May of 1997, and we were in the mountains west of Nha Trang in Vietnam. We were scheduled to move back to Houston, Texas, in the summer of 1997. In January, during a school break, we had gone on a several week trip to Australia, as promised. I had felt that, since Vietnam was only an hour plane ride away, why not go back and have a look before heading home? Patsy thought it was a good idea, and Lisa was game. When we landed at the airport at Saigon, now Ho Chi Minh City, it looked exactly like it had when I flew out of there in 1970. Quonset huts still lined the runway, there were berms of sandbags built to protect the terminal building from rocket and mortar fire, and the building itself looked like a relic. Exactly the same! We had become used to the modern, bustling cities of Kuala Lumpur, Singapore, and Bangkok. The contrast was stark and, in my opinion, showed just how badly South Vietnam had suf- fered after the war.

I had hired a car to try to find my old base camp out in the mountains west of Nha Trang. The driver was young and did not remember anything from the war years. I tried to direct him but with limited success. I definitely recognized landmarks like the large statue of the Virgin Mary on one of the mountaintops. However, after much searching, it became apparent that the base had been reclaimed by the jungle, never to be seen again. It was an emotional journey for me but far less so for Patsy and Lisa. I guess it was one of those things where you had to be there, and if you weren't, you didn't understand.

The young people we met in Vietnam were extremely friendly and happy to talk to the Americans, even sell us some trinkets! They couldn't remember the war and the pain that came with it. The older people who had to attend "reeducation" camps were sad over the lost decades of their lives. Many of them had been prosperous shopkeepers or farmers before the war but now had to eke out a living driving cabs or selling their wares to tourists.

After a few years as exploration manager in Malaysia, I was getting restless and ready to move on. However, after all of our previous moves, we did not want to make Lisa move while she was still in high school and let the powers that be know that. So after four years in Malaysia, Lisa graduated from the International School of Kuala Lumpur, and we all headed back to Houston. Patsy had not wanted to leave Texas for this side of the world, but after spending the past four years settling in and enjoying all that Malaysia had to offer, it was hard going back.

We had watched the city transform in many ways over these four years. A small example would be Santa Claus. Each year that we were in KL, the department stores began to celebrate Christmas a little more. Santa Claus began showing up in shop windows, sometimes even with his reindeer. The country may have been Muslim, but the merchants knew that gift giving meant sales. Another example was the rapid development of new buildings and shopping malls. An old British racetrack was demolished to make room for a large park surrounded by new office buildings.

The Esso building was directly across from the PETRONAS Twin Towers—at the time of their construction the tallest buildings in the world. I was able to watch their entire construction from my office window. A joint Malaysian-South Korean Company constructed one tower, and a joint Malaysian-Japanese company built the other. Each company was forced by the government to have a Malaysian partner, but this was really a South Korea-versus-Japan effort. From the beginning, the competition was readily apparent. Construction went on day and night, causing an alarming number of construction mishaps and deaths during the work. Over twenty construction workers lost their lives. This great bustle of construction activity halted when each tower was about halfway up. What happened? Measurements by a government inspector had determined that one of the towers was leaning by an unacceptable amount. Apparently, the rush of the work was taking its toll. At this point, the prime minister declared that each of the South Korean and Japanese companies would be declared joint winners and that there would be no more racing to the top.

12

Back to Houston: Round 3

Patsy and I were moving back to Houston for the third time as a couple in July of 1997. With all of our practice, we should have had it down, but this turned out to be our hardest move. Lisa was going off to college, so we were trying to figure out how to move into a house without her. Patsy had an especially hard time with that because of how close the two of them were through all of these moves. There was also the reverse culture adjustment. The daily rush of KL and the Royal Selangor Gold Club were no more. I was coming back and trying to figure out what the rest of my career at Exxon was going to look like. In hindsight, it seems like a very uninspiring time in our lives, though the adjustments we made were important for the next chapters.

In Malaysia, we had taken time over two summers to take Lisa on college tours. We mainly went up and down the east coast as that seemed to be the thing to do. Of all places, a recruiter from Franklin and Marshall had come through Kuala Lumpur and visited with Lisa the summer before her senior year of college. She had not been blown away by any of the colleges we visited, so applications were sent all over. We barely got them filled out in time. I can remember rushing to the post office to get it sent out in time and feeling like I was trying to catch that school bus through the cornfield again. After the acceptances, it came down to Dad's alma mater, and she enrolled there in the fall of 1997.

When we were in Kuala Lumpur, F&M did not seem so far away. But having arrived back in Houston, we realized that Lancaster was quite distant. Patsy and I drove her up together, and over the next four years, we shared that drive with Lisa many times. Although she was technically away from home for the first time, Lisa had travelled the world, and it did not seem like such a big deal for either her or us. In fact, her experiences in high school travelling to other countries for meets and such were so different that she, being a bit shy and unpretentious to begin with, found it difficult to share with her friends.

The house with the fishpond was in our rear view mirror! After having lived in two far-flung suburbs of Houston, we decided to try to locate more centrally this time. We wanted to be closer to our friends and all of the attractions of the city. By this time, Houston had become a worldly city. We settled on a nice townhouse in the Tanglewood area, just north of the Galleria shopping complex. Even then my Pennsylvania Dutch penny-pinching came out as I originally had my sights on a smaller version in a less desirable neighborhood. Patsy stood in the middle of the street in front of the one we eventually purchased and stated that she would accept nothing less!

The house was still under construction, so we were able to customize it to a certain extent. Unfortunately, there wasn't space for a fishpond. An IRS tax rule created a slight complication in the whole process. When you sell your primary residence, you have three years to put the money into your next house, or you pay a capital gains tax. If you go overseas, you have four years. We were coming in right at the deadline by the time we came back from Malaysia, and I asked our tax accountant what I should do. He informed me that we could buy the house, but to show that it was a primary residence, I needed to sleep there at least a few nights and prepare some meals as well. So I dutifully spent a few nights in a sleeping bag on the third floor of the framed up house and heated a couple meals over a camp stove. Patsy said she would join me when the house was completely finished, thank you very much.

Patsy was feeling quite down with Lisa gone. She focused much of her energy during this time period on making the house into a home for us all. It took several years for Patsy to be fully pleased with her efforts, but when she was finished, the house was truly beautiful.

I had always harbored the ambition that, having left the farm, gone against my parents and gone to Vietnam, I might as well make the whole effort worthwhile by going for the moon. To me, this had translated into achieving a very senior level, or even the highest level, at Exxon. Now to any reasonable person with knowledge of the situation, this would have come across as patently laughable. First of all, as a trained geologist, I was in the wrong field—engineers had led Exxon for decades. Secondly, having taken sidetracks to serve in the army and get an advanced degree, I had started way too late on the corporate ladder to be considered for that role. I had also spent a large portion of my career at Exxon in the action-oriented

Production Department. Exxon placed a lot of focus on being a functionally organized company; engineers ran production and geologists ran exploration. In their eyes, I was a man without a country. However, it was just like Dad telling me I couldn't do something. It didn't stop me from trying. In this effort, Patsy was both supportive and pragmatic, encouraging me while making sure that I was viewing the situation realistically. I had asked her to move to literally the ends of the earth for my career—I'm including Kingsville as well as Kuala Lumpur. One of the results of my having spent so much time in production is that I had more close friends there than in exploration, including Rex Tillerson.

After our return from Malaysia, Patsy and Renda were talking on the phone, and Renda relayed that Rex had created a bit of a stir among the Exxon hierarchy by turning down an overseas assignment. Renda revealed that the primary reason was her objection. You can imagine how Patsy must have felt. But she never held this against me—neither making me feel bad because I had made this sacrifice and had not been rewarded nor reminding me that she had been willing to go, but Renda had not. She was totally a sport about it. As I said, she recognized the reality of the situation a lot more clearly than myself. Although I considered Rex a friend of mine and clearly appreciated his talent, I was a bit chagrinned later when he became Chairman of Exxon in spite of not having run all legs of the marathon. However, I also learned a valuable lesson, although a bit late in life, to enjoy the journey not just looking at the destination. It is like the Pennsylvania Dutch saying, "We grown so soon old and so late smart!"

*****

My new position with Exxon was manager of New Venture Development in the Exploration Department. It gave me a lot of responsibility and freedom but was pretty much a dead end career wise. I was fifty and not eligible for retirement for five more years, but leaving before retirement would have meant leaving a lot of money on the table. Thus, Patsy would have made the sacrifices of moving and still be faced with returning groceries! I felt trapped but knew that I needed to stick it out and make the best of the situation. Patsy understood my disappointment and pretty much took the tack that Exxon had screwed up and given me a bum deal. For this, she recited numerous examples, but I must say she always had the highest regard for Rex—and if there was one thing that Patsy was good at, it was judging character.

We decided that we would make the most of the next five years. I did this to the best of my ability at the office, coming up with new ideas and continuing to travel. In 2000, I became the first Exxon executive to travel to Iran since the overthrow of the Shah. Exxon saw a window of opportunity opening there as the political situation was changing, so I spent a week at a conference in Tehran meeting various dignitaries. Exxon, in their typical conservative fashion, sent an attorney with me to make sure that I did not say anything that would have gotten the company (or me) in trouble.

On the flight from London to Tehran, I was sitting beside an Iranian man who complained, as he ordered a whiskey from the stewardess, that the only place he could drink was on the airplane, because at his home in London his wife would not let him drink and at his place of business in Tehran the government would not let him drink. Another hip pocket guy.

What was really starting to bother Patsy is that over the years, all of the moving, travelling, and adjusting to new cultural surroundings had made the three of us very close. We referred to ourselves as the "Three Musketeers." But with Lisa off at college and with me planning to leave Exxon, the Musketeers were drifting apart. Patsy filled her newfound time with golf—sweeping the competition after all of those hours on the driving range in Malaysia. Patsy loved playing with the ladies during the week, and she and I continued the tradition we had started in Malaysia of playing together on Sunday afternoons.

It might be an overstatement to say that we spent this period of our life wandering aimlessly about. However, because neither of us was living where we grew up and because we had lived in so many places by this point, I think we were searching for rootedness. We felt a bit like vagabonds. We did take great satisfaction in finding a church home at St. Martin's Episcopal, a few blocks from our house. We made regular visits to see Patsy's sister Sharon, who with her husband Jerry had a lovely home on a golf course at Reynolds's Plantation east of Atlanta, Georgia. Jerry, Patsy, and I would frequently play a round of golf together. We loved going to see the Houston Symphony. However, when the discussion came to, "Where do we go from here?" we came up empty.

Patsy loved the situation at Reynolds Plantation, and we bought a building lot there thinking about a part-time retirement home. I explained to Patsy that, while I loved golf, I would have a difficult time living in a place where that was the only thing to do. Some people are blessed with the ability of enjoying life as it exists—smelling the roses, planting their garden, and feeling the gentle breezes in the air—that, however, would not be me. I always feel like I need to be "doing something." I had yet to figure out what that something was, and when we talked about places to live besides Houston or Reynolds, we came up empty every time.

13

New Beginnings

In September of 2002, I listened as one of the members from the Greens and Grounds committee at BraeBurn Country Club, a nearly scratch golfer, told the tale of his round the previous weekend. Every country club has a policy on how to place the rakes back in the bunkers after using them. Some say in the bunkers, some say outside the bunkers. The golf pro at BraeBurn advocated a policy of placing the business end of the rake in the bunker, with the handle laying on the edge so that it could be reached without having to walk into the bunker. On the ninth hole at BraeBurn, a straight par 5, easy for good golfers, there is a bunker guarding the green on the left side. This is the only obstacle preventing one from rolling the ball up onto the green. I was listening as the committee member complained that he had hit a beautiful shot and was going to be on the green in two, but someone had left the handle of a rake too far extended outside the bunker, and his ball had hit the rake handle, knocking it into the bunker. From this ensued a thirty-minute discussion among the committee about just how the rakes should be placed in the bunkers and how we were going to communicate this to the members. Thirty minutes on rakes in the bunkers. I was fifty-five years old at the time and would reasonably be expected to live another twenty years or so. I said to myself, "Davey Boy, you are going to have to think of doing something better to do than this for the next twenty years."

*****

I had taken early retirement from Exxon on March 28, 2002. In the back of my mind, I held the idea that I might want to end up running my own oil exploration company. There were several reasons not to jump into that pool without checking the depth of the water. I had no clue where to start. Working for Exxon had certainly been a challenge and a full-time job, but as an executive, I had been pampered in a lot of ways. My only familiarity with the computer was how to send and receive e-mails. Getting funding for profitable projects had never been an issue. Riding out oil price booms and busts was just like going across the ocean on a large luxury liner; one hardly noticed waves that might swamp a smaller vessel.

123

During the last five years of my Exxon career, I had carefully watched colleagues and friends as they transitioned from working for large oil-and-gas companies. Most went quietly away, bought a retirement home, spent time with their families, and learned how to place rakes in the bunkers. Those who did try a career transition mainly made a hash of it. My observation was that they tried to jump from being an officer of a large cruise liner onto a small boat and continue to act like they were the officer of a large cruise liner. Exxon was a command and control outfit like nothing I have ever seen—and I have witnessed the command structure of the US Army, academia, and the Mennonite Church! As an executive in Exxon, when you say jump, your subordinates ask, "How high?" on their way up. On the other hand, everyone in the executive ranks had started at the ground level and worked their way up to that. I believed that to be successful; one would have to start at the ground level of that smaller vessel and work up the same way. This was not an easy adjustment for the men who tried, and it accounted for an almost 100 percent dropout rate among those attempting.

Another bit of invaluable advice came from an unlikely source. In the summer of 2002, soon after my retirement, Patsy and I went to New York for the wedding of Nicole Glanville. She is the daughter of Jim and Jill, Lisa's godparents. A reception party was being held in an old beautifully renovated brownstone house in the Lower East Side, and I found myself talking with a retired attorney. When he asked me what I was going to do, I said that I was not sure but that if I did anything in the work world again, it would have to be my own company. I was not going to go to work for anyone else at this point. His advice was that if I was considering this I should read *Into Thin Air* by Jon Krakauer. It is a story of a climb up Mt. Everest that went terribly wrong. It took me a while to figure out how this book related to starting a business, but then it hit me. The lower part of the climb up Everest is a long relatively easy slope. Experienced and knowledgeable climbers take their time and use this to gradually ease in and get acclimated. Amateurs would say, "Hey, this is easy," and go jogging across it, only to have it catch up with them later as they never properly acclimated. So I said to myself, "When the time comes, start at the bottom, and take it slow until you figure out what you are doing."

Soon after retirement, I was greeted by some not-so-good news on a visit to my physician. My PSA (sign of possible prostate issues, including cancer) was high, and he suggested a visit to an urologist for further testing. The biopsy came back negative, but he was still concerned and suggested that I come back later in the year.

Retirement was an entirely new adjustment. We were moving into a stage of life that we planned on staying in. We played golf, but I could not get into that as an everyday event, as many successful retirees seem to be able to do. We both enjoyed travelling, but I did not want to splurge on any large trips until I saw firsthand how the finances were going to come together. We bought Patsy a new car, so I suggested we take a couple of "land cruises" while we settled into retirement and thought about the possibility of not so good results from a redo of the biopsy.

We drove to Reynolds Plantation to visit Sharon and Jerry and play some golf. After that, we headed west for a trip, which took about six weeks. First was a stop at Red Lodge, Montana, for a one-week stay under a Franklin and Marshall College alumni program. The retreat was held at a camp used by the geology students for summer field studies and could be generously described as "rustic." The days were spent on looking at the beautiful scenery, listening to lectures, and taking hikes in the mountains. The issue, and a talking point for years to come, was the accommodations. The small cabins had no running water or bathroom facilities. An outdoor toilet was a hundred yards up a trail through the woods. I paced off the a hundred yards because I knew that if I did not verify the distance, it would be two miles by the time the story got back to Houston! Patsy encountered one other Southern Belle on the retreat, and the two of them regaled themselves with alternative versions of how to describe the facilities.

From Montana, we drove north for a few nights and several days of golf at the Banff Springs Hotel. Thankfully, at this beautiful resort in the Canadian Rockies, they did have running water and in-room bathroom facilities! From there, we drove west across

Canada and down the Pacific Coast and stopped to see my brother Tom and his family at their ranch east of Portland, Oregon. We continued down the California coast, went east to the Grand Canyon, and then went on to Sonora, Arizona, Taos, New Mexico and several places in between. It was a trip filled with wonderful memories.

On our return to Houston, I was greeted with an urgent letter from my urologist imploring me to come in for another biopsy. By February of 2003, Patsy and I were both shaken by the diagnosis of the cancer. Patsy decided that the best way to deal with the news would be by doing meditation; she even tried to amplify its effects by doing it standing on her head in the closet. Mainly, it resulted in a slight rotator cuff tear that would bother her for several years.

After looking at the options, we opted for surgery, which was performed in March 2003. Recovery took months, and needless to say was not much fun. But here I sit fifteen years later, with no reoccurrence.

By the summer of 2003, I was feeling better. I had had my "rake in the bunker" epiphany and was starting to look around to see how I might occupy myself. PWJ Woods was a retired Exxon exploration manager I had met, obviously, through work. He and a friend of his were starting up a new E&P (exploration and production) company and asked me to come and tag along. PWJ, or Jim as his friends called him, was about seventy-five years old at the time, and his friend was the same age. Jim was from the UK, and I never actually found out what the "PWJ" stood for; at Exxon, he was frequently called (not to his face) "Alphabet" Woods. Jim's friend was a former independent oil-and-gas producer who had built up a rather large company back in the roaring 1980s and was back for another go at it. I thought that this was the perfect situation for me as I could learn the business from these wizened veterans. Patsy had always been a reliable source of advice and guidance for me, and she did not like either one of these guys from the jump.

She said that they were four flushers. I did not know this term before, but it derives from a poker hand called a flush, which is five cards of one suit. If someone routinely has only four cards of a suit and tries to convince you that he has a flush, he is said to be a four flusher. I hung around these guys for six months before I figured out that their idea of a business partnership was that I would do all the work and they would get all the money. Patsy was right—she had always said that teaching second grade had taught her how to judge who the little devils in the room were!

*****

For the next four years, we continued my slow start up Mt. Everest with some normal retirement activities. Besides our normal golfing at BraeBurn, we would take short road trips interspersed with at least one large trip each year. A Mediterranean cruise, a trip to Spain to see Lisa on her junior year abroad, and a safari trip to South Africa. Another favorite pastime became going to the gym and working out together. Patsy had always kept herself in good shape, and so we decided to fend off father time by doing it together.

A former Exxon geologist, Rick, had worked in my group in Kingsville, Texas, and kept in touch with me over the years. He claimed to have some good prospects in a geological basin called the DJ Basin east of Denver, Colorado. One weekend, when Patsy was away visiting one of her sisters and mother, I asked Rick to come to Houston and show them to me. We rolled his maps and logs out on the kitchen table and inspected them. I was pretty impressed. The prospects certainly had potential, so I decided to pursue the idea further.

First, I took Rick's hand-drawn prospects to be properly drafted so they would look presentable to an investor. I asked friends around town where I could find a draftsman similar to those we had at Exxon, and they laughed. "Dave," they said, "nobody does that anymore. Now people draw their maps up on a computer, hit print, and voila, it comes out drafted." So I decided that I would enter the modern world and learn how to draft on the computer. It was shockingly difficult. I bought the computer software program and tried to teach myself how to use it but relied heavily on the help desk. Sometimes I would call them twenty times a day. I ended up signing up for a one-week course on the program. I learned—I was not a pro—but I could get by. My climb definitely slowed around this time, but I was slowly making my way up!

I had generated a bit of interest from a few others in the prospects. John Harms, a friend from Littleton, Colorado, joined me as my first partner in the project. We used John's office in Denver as a meeting place, and I would commute there once every month. In the meantime, I had started using a small bedroom in our home for an office, graduating after about a year into a larger bedroom on the third floor. Lisa had just graduated and taken a job in Dallas working for an insurance company. After a year, she informed me that insurance was boring and she wanted to try something else. I insisted that she stay for at least two years to establish a bit of a track record. In 2003, she left her insurance job and moved back to Houston. By this point, I was working by myself on the computer and commuting to Denver. I had recently put together a large project using Excel that had taken me about a week to create. On reviewing it with John, I realized that I had made a mistake and would have to completely redo it. Lisa was between jobs, and I was dreading the redo, so I asked if she would give me a hand. She was a whiz at the computer, and we had it redone, correctly, in two days. Soon after that, I asked Lisa if she would come work with me. She asked for how long, and I said I would prefer three to five years. She stayed for fourteen.

At about the time that Lisa came to work, the home office was getting a bit small. Patsy was tired of strangers in pickup trucks stopping by to discuss the oil business, and the visitors were only increasing because business was picking up. I leased a real office in a building a few blocks from our house.

Up until 2005, the funding for the business had come primarily from me, with John pitching in a smaller percent. Around this time, Exxon made a change in their rules for vesting of stock options and allowed me to benefit from the Exxon stock appreciation for up to ten years, rather than the previously allowed five. Patsy did keep a close eye on what I was doing, but by now she had come to trust that she wouldn't have to send any groceries back.

John and I began dabbling in buying actual oil-and-gas leases. By 2005, it was clear that a revolution was taking place in the US oil-and-gas business. It had been triggered by the innovative combination of precision steered horizontal drilling of wells and multistage hydraulic fracturing (colloquially called fracking). George Mitchell, a Greek immigrant in Texas, had first developed fracking. He used it to drill into tight gas rocks in the Fort Worth Basin in the 1990s. For years, it was thought to be applicable only to gas deposits and used for the gas developments in the Eagle Ford Shale of South Texas and the Fayetteville Shale of Arkansas. In 2004, the Bakken of North Dakota started development. The Bakken development contained oil within the rock, and the new technology demonstrated that it could work for oil production as well as natural gas.

John and I thought that the oil productive Niobrara formation in the DJ Basin would be equally suitable for this technology and sought to assemble an acreage position in it. With the promise of some financial backing from a company in the area, we had nominated a large block of state acreage. The federal and state governments own a lot of the mineral rights in the country, and every quarter they hold lease sales. You nominate pieces of land that you would like to lease from them to explore. A few weeks before the state lease auction, the company needed to back us dropped out.

I had my back to the wall and did not know what to do. I had already invested almost a million dollars of our retirement money and knew that I shouldn't risk anymore. I approached several friends around Houston: real estate and insurance executives, entrepreneurs, and some geologists; they said they would help back me. I was definitely on a steep learning curve with this exercise and needed a limited partnership as fast as possible to pull this off. I spent the next couple of weeks running around Houston like I had hot coals under my feet getting everything put together in time for the big state lease sale. Lisa was a great help, and we pulled it off, buying a large amount of acreage at an extremely low cost. I was starting up the mountain.

Over the next two years, I put together two more limited partnerships for the purpose of leasing this play. In a limited partnership, one buys an interest in the company. I made pitches to friends-and-family-type investors to gather the funds. A general partner leads the whole endeavor and has total control over all of the money and decision-making. It is called a limited partnership because exposure is limited for the other investors, but they have no control once their money is invested. If someone were to sue the company, a limited partner's exposure is only as large as their investment, but no limit is placed on their profit margins. I was the general partner in these arrangements, and I'm sure that Patsy had no idea that she would be getting into this in her retirement years. Nonetheless, she would come to these meetings and cheer me on with a big smile on her face. The wives of some of my investors would see Patsy at parties or a restaurant and corner her to ask, "Do you think that Dave knows what he is doing?" Of course she always gave me a ringing endorsement, even though she was wondering the same thing herself!

By the summer of 2006, we had accumulated a large amount of acreage. I decided that it was time to get some real funding based on this and started climbing the mountain at a faster pace. In February, I secured backing from a large private equity firm and was finally able to start running a small oil-and-gas firm without raiding the retirement account. By the summer of 2007, we were continuing to acquire oil-and-gas leases and started drilling a few vertical test wells. Things were starting to go along pretty well.

In early 2007, Patsy and I found out about a new type of cruise with a company called Kalos Golf. We would cruise down the Rhine River, playing golf every other day at courses in Austria, Germany, Hungary, and the Czech Republic. Sightseeing was scheduled every other day. We signed up for the October 2007 cruise and had a blast. Life was good.

PART 4

The Diagnosis

14

Unaccompanied

December 6, 2016

I sat staring out the window at the heavy snowfall amidst a beautiful wooded mountain scene. A friend had loaned me his house in Frisco, Colorado, for a few days to get away. I didn't want to talk to anyone. I just needed to be alone with my thoughts. I needed to mourn. I had buried Patsy on November 29, 2016, a week before. The burst of activity that comes from the many demands of this had settled down—and I was alone.

My Patsy is gone. Aloud, and silently, I repeated it, echoing through the house and my hollow self. Announcing the obvious to the recesses of my brain that had yet to fully process this reality. Despite my doing virtually nothing else for two days but telling myself this, it was not sinking in. I simply could not believe it. How did I get here?

15

Rolling to the Rockies

In the fall of 2008, Patsy and I were touring the ancient part of Salzburg, Austria, seeing where Beethoven lived and admiring the old stone throughout the city. We spent our days eating in the local restaurants, exploring the historic city, and playing golf on the local course. There are always cultural differences between countries, but it was interesting to see how they were expressed on the Austrian golf course. The courses were a bit more rugged, with no paved cart paths or halfway houses for a snack after the ninth hole. The scenery more than compensated for the extra effort, and the gorgeous weather topped off a grand day. The course was set in a valley between rather high hills, and it gave it the real Austrian feel. Patsy and I were celebrating thirty years together on this trip. After the disaster, which was my first foray into marital commitment, I told Patsy before we got married that my goal was to make it thirty years, and I thought it might take a miracle to get there—but here we were!

The cruise down the Rhine was idyllic. Although we did not have television or newspapers, there were folks on board who were telephoning home, and we did get snippets of information from the crew. The financial system was in full meltdown. It created a rather surreal feeling, as we cruised down the Rhine, basking in the lovely sights created by the high mountains along the river and the quaint villages tucked into the valleys. Nothing felt like it was falling apart there.

The tour continued in Budapest and included impressive visits to the old Imperial Palace and living quarters, mixed in with tales of how things had been during the Second World War and under Communist rule. Our visit to the Jewish Quarter stayed with us the longest. We were brought to the display of the "shoes" on the banks of the river, symbolizing the many Jews who had been driven into the river to drown during the war.

From Budapest, we took the train to Prague, in the Czech Republic, for a tour of that beautiful city and another round of golf. In Prague, they referred to the "velvet glove" of Communism, as many of the more strident aspects were not as severely enforced. I even remember one of the tour guides lamenting that she was worried about her retirement savings and speculating (seriously) that under the Communists she wouldn't have had to worry about that. Unbelievable and quite a different tale than anything we heard in Hungary. We marked our thirtieth anniversary on a high note, but when we returned to Houston, our lives took a more somber turn on several counts.

The first week back, I had headed to Denver to see how things were progressing with the business. I called home that first evening, and Patsy reported that she had a wonderful day playing golf with friends from BraeBurn. The golf she had played on the trip helped her game, and she was clearly on a high. Two days later, still in the office in Denver, I got a call from Lisa. Patsy was feeling badly and had been taken to the hospital. The preliminary diagnosis was pneumonia, but they were still running tests. She recovered and was able to come home after another few days, but she had developed a cough and couldn't seem to get her energy back. This was to be the start of a multiyear struggle.

At the office, I was also getting an ominous feeling. The financial crisis was devastating all sectors, and my investors were clearly nervous. They were cutting back on funding and sending a clear signal that future funding for the company may be in jeopardy.

Through the rest of 2008 and the first half of 2009, we struggled to get a more clear diagnosis and treatment for Patsy's illness. We had consulted several pulmonologists, and they were treating her for a viral lung infection with Prednisone. It was making her feel sluggish, and she was not improving. Finally, I insisted on another opinion and suggested to her primary pulmonologist that perhaps we should visit the Mayo or Cleveland clinics. He strongly suggested that we try National Jewish Health in Denver. According to him, and now I would concur, it was the preeminent hospital in the world for lung issues. This was also convenient as I had a small condominium in Denver for when I went there on business.

It took several visits, many tests, and almost a year; but by mid-2010, National Jewish had a diagnosis: mycobacterial avium complex, or MAC for short. It was a bacterial infection in the lungs, sometimes referred to as atypical tuberculosis. Part of the atypical part is that it is not transmittable. What causes this? What had brought this on? The doctors were not able to answer either of those questions. The bacteria that had infected Patsy's lungs was common and can be generally found floating in the air. It infects some people and not others for unknown reasons. The doctors at National Jewish, having seen many cases of this from all over the United States, could only say that the most common group of people to be infected were "thin white women from the South." The climate is more humid in the South, but why the rest? I began to think—could Patsy's lungs have been weakened by that first case of pneumonia she contracted in Malaysia? Could this have been a factor triggering this infection? Questions swirled in my head, and I wasn't sure if I would ever find their answers.

The prescribed cure was a cocktail of three very strong antibiotics. We started this regimen and continued to go back to National Jewish Health every three months for monitoring. The treatment seemed to be working, albeit slowly.

Meanwhile, things were continuing to be challenging at the office. My investors, Natural Gas Partners, or NGP, had never really understood the exploration play I had taken to them. They had funded me because Lee Raymond recommended me. Lee had been the chairman of Exxon when I worked there, and one of his sons, Colin, recommended me to his father. NGP wanted production and PUDs, not exploration acreage. PUDs are proven undeveloped locations; they are low-risk drilling opportunities that are located next to proven locations. After getting funding from NGP, we purchased the Fort Collins Oil Field northwest of Denver along with several smaller oil fields.

Our leased acreage had grown to about 160,000 acres, mostly exploration, and things had been moving smoothly until the financial crisis. After that, NGP began to rethink and contract. They were getting ready to do what I have since learned is called a Trash Compactor. At the time, NGP had five companies funded in the Rocky Mountain area. The plan was to consolidate the companies by firing the staff of four and moving the assets into one company. Well, this is America, so they can fire you, but they can't steal from you. At the time, the management team, my friends, family partners, and I had 20 percent of the capital invested, while NGP had 80 percent. Their plan was to give us a 20 percent interest in all of the properties. The problem in the oil business is that you can't really do anything with a 20 percent interest except ride along and watch the majority owner do what they wish.

I did not think that the production and PUDs (potential drill locations located near producing wells) had much upside, but I still believed strongly in the exploration play in the Niobrara in DJ Basin, where John and I had originally targeted. I went to NGP in December of 2008 with a proposal: let me have all the exploration acreage, and I would give them all of the current production and the PUD wells. They balked at this. While they did not really understand what I was doing and had no desire to fund further efforts, they were wondering in the back of their minds if I was right. After six months of negotiating, in the early summer of 2009, I closed a deal with NGP structured almost exactly as I had proposed it to them. So in June of 2009, I had the exploration acreage I wanted, my staff (five including myself, Lisa, a CFO, a geologist and an engineer), no debt, and six months of working capital, but no cash flow. It was a long summer.

A company named EOG had drilled a horizontal exploration well in the summer of 2009, right in the middle of our acreage holdings. The results were kept confidential for a while, but by the end of the year, word was out. It was the most prolific well ever drilled in the DJ Basin! The results set off a land rush in the DJ Basin the likes of which had not been seen in the Rocky Mountains since the Gold Rush. I did not have the capital, the staff, or the experience to drill in the Basin; and so we sold our acreage. Sales of various plots were sold to ten different companies over a period of about six months during the first half of 2010. Since NGP had bowed out, the friends and family investors, myself, and the rest of the management team had each made a twelve times return on the money invested. Patsy no longer had to answer the question, "Does Dave know what he is doing?"

So in one shot, I had made almost double the money I had left Exxon with after twenty-seven years. I felt invincible. I thought that this was not so difficult, and I could probably do it again (con-

veniently forgetting how tough it had been in late 2008). I decided
that it was no fun getting the rug pulled out from underneath me as
NGP had done. I would use my earnings and have a go of it on my
own. I believed in this Niobrara play and thought I understood it.
Through a friend, I had made the acquaintance of a rancher who had
a ten-thousand-acre spread in Laramie County, Wyoming, which I
thought would be an attractive area. During the fall of 2010 and the
spring of 2011, I obtained a lease on the ranch and commissioned
a 3D seismic survey. Unfortunately, in early 2011, a horizontal test
well was drilled near the ranch with disappointing results. This was
not looking good. By spring 2011, I had not only used up just about
all the money I had made, but the acreage seemed to be turning into
a bad investment.

Patsy was *furious* with me!

Fortunately, by September 2011, I had located an investor
group willing to not only back me going forward but allowed me
to take most of my money off the table. This left me with a size-
able investment and guaranteed that I wouldn't lose everything I had
made. I breathed a sigh of relief, and Patsy forgave me!

Patsy's treatment for her MAC progressed well during this time.
She was feeling much better, and the doctors at National Jewish proclaimed that her follow-up exams were showing good progress. We
began to discuss the possibility of another long trip. We had received
a brochure in the mail from the University of Texas alumni association advertising a trip called "Around the World by Private Jet." It
described a nine-country, twenty-one-day trip visiting places such as
the Taj Mahal, Angkor Wat, and the Pyramids of Giza. The "private
jet" turned out to be a Boeing 757 especially outfitted to carry about
seventy people, instead of the usual 233. I was immediately convinced that we should do this. Patsy was a bit more cautious—how
does one dress and pack for such a trip?

The doctors felt that Patsy should continue taking her antibiotics until the end of 2011, but they did clear her.

What a ride. The trip was like taking a limousine ride around
the world. Everything was handled beforehand. No waiting for one's
hotel key to be handed out by a slow-moving clerk filling out lots

of forms. No waiting in line for passport control, they had been stamped and the passport safeguarded for the next stop (everywhere except for Australia, a stickler for no exceptions to misery). Each stop usually involved landing at about three in the afternoon, a bus ride to the hotel, during which we were given a talk on the local area, along with about ten dollars' worth of local currency for tipping (typically in a locally bought small craft bag). The first night would be a dinner at the hotel or another local restaurant; it was almost always local cuisine, commonly accompanied with a performance by a local dance or singing group. The next morning would generally feature breakfast followed by a bus tour of the local area accompanied by lectures and walking tours.

The stops were incredible. We had an exclusive train ride from Cusco, Peru, to the ancient Inca ruins at Machu Picchu. Then on to Easter Island and those magnificent statues. A stop in American Samoa and the Great Barrier Reef of Australia for some snorkeling and a trip through the Northeastern Australian rainforest. Angkor Wat in Cambodia is a place we probably should have visited when we were living in Malaysia but didn't. The ancient ruins in the middle of a rainforest took our breath away. The Taj Mahal was our favorite stop. The Great Migration on the Serengeti Plain was a sight to behold for sure. Then to the ancient ruins of Luxor, Egypt, and a day stop to visit the pyramids. The final stop was a visit to the old city of Fez, Morocco—not a favorite of Patsy's—a few too many pungent smells!

On our return to Houston, we were in a pretty good mood—buoyed not only by our travels but also by the fact that Patsy seemed to be fully recovered from the MAC infection.

In January of 2012, my company, with our new investors, drilled a vertical test well on the Polo Ranch acreage that I had leased in Wyoming. We made a small oil well in a deeper formation, precluding it from being called an outright "dry hole," but the core we took in the Niobrara did not look good. We had the geology wrong on our key play. It was back to the drawing boards.

As the summer of 2012 approached, I explained to Patsy that, although I still had confidence in our investment in the new company, we had stumbled out of the starting gate. I felt that spending more time in Denver to oversee the venture would be our best chance of success. I asked if she would consider buying a second home in Denver and spending more time up there. We drove to Denver in May of 2012. On the way, we made an overnight stop along the freeway just outside of Oklahoma City, Oklahoma. We were in a fleabag hotel and could not find a good restaurant nearby, so we ended up eating some Whataburger hamburgers in our car and finished listening to a book on tape that we had started during the day as we drove. It was quite different from the trip around the world, but we enjoyed each other's company and frequently reminisced about how fun the evening was. In June, we bought a condominium on the top floor of a complex in Cherry Creek, on the south side of Denver. The location was great, and the view was fantastic. However, the décor was not up to Southern Belle specs. We spent the summer in the condo, using cardboard boxes for most of the furniture, and began renovations in the fall.

16

The Tells

Late on a relaxing Sunday afternoon, I popped out to the store and when I arrived back home, I found Patsy in the middle of the den floor, lying facedown, unable to get up. She had fallen as she got up to go to the kitchen.

A few days later, I was in the office when I received a call from Nick, our dog walker. "Dave, I just wanted to let you know that when I arrived here Patsy was lying on the floor. She seems better now but a little shaken up. I'm staying for a little longer to make sure she's okay."

A while after that, I came home early from the office and found Patsy downstairs on the driveway. Her face was covered with blood, and passersby were helping her get cleaned up. She had been taking our dog Hannah for a walk, and Hannah had pulled hard on her leash, causing Patsy to fall facefirst onto the sidewalk. She said that she felt okay, but I insisted that we go the emergency room. Sixteen stiches were required on her eyebrow.

From the time we went on the trip around the world in late 2011 until the summer of 2013, Patsy had appeared to be in good health. She was not playing golf as much, but that was because she underwent rotator cuff surgery in 2012, and it never healed properly. In hindsight, I think that this was an early precursor to her eventual physical downfall. She still walked regularly, and we often walked together, but the social as well as physical aspect of golf was never truly replaced.

From the time we bought the Denver condo in June of 2012, Patsy had been working on a plan to get the place up to "Southern Belle specs." The work we decided to do on the Denver condo was really a full renovation. We stripped everything to the studs and built it back up. I spent the winter of 2012 through 2013 working in the Denver office during the week and commuting to Houston on the weekends.

The high point, or perhaps the low point I should say, of my winter stay in Denver happened one evening, when I stepped out to take stock of the weather. It was windy and about eight degrees Fahrenheit, the sliding door to my small condo slammed behind me, and I was locked out on the small patio. I had on my office clothes, which were good for winter weather, but not for a long night of it! My cell phone was back inside, and the weather meant that few people were around. I tried everything to bring attention to my plight. I threw a seat cushion at a passing car, but the wind carried it away, and the car drove on. Eventually, I got the attention of a maintenance man at a nearby building and convinced him to call 911. The fire department responded with a large retrieval vehicle, and four fire fighters came through the condo door to rescue me—after I convinced them that I was not a cat burglar!

Patsy has done a beautiful job with the design of the condo. Yet again, she had created a home for us. I thought the place could be on the cover of a magazine. It was a soft French design, elegant and light, with a patio that gave us a view of the Rockies. Even though I felt it was great, I was still a bit nervous when Patsy came up in June of 2013 for her first look. She also proclaimed it beautiful—I had passed the Southern Belle exam!

We enjoyed the summer of 2013 in our new place. A number of visitors came, and we had a good time taking them on trips to the mountains and exploring new restaurants in Denver. Patsy even proclaimed at one point that she was beginning to like Denver. However, it was during this time that she began to have these falling episodes. She was always good-natured about them, even when she lay for an hour or so until someone came to her rescue. I was beginning to worry about how often they were happening, so we started visiting various neurologists to figure out the cause.

Meanwhile, my reason for wanting to spend more time in Denver was starting to pay off. After drilling that early dry hole, we had gone back to the drawing boards and come up with a more reliable geologic model for the DJ Basin. Based on this, our investors had approved purchase of a block of acreage from the Chesapeake company as they began to exit the basin plays.

This was truly an extraordinary time to be an exploration geologist in the oil-and-gas business. The horizontal drilling and fracking technology in the early 2000s had set off a new gold rush as companies of all sizes sought to buy oil-and-gas leases and utilize the technology to find and develop new plays. Around 2004, the discovery of new plays was slowing down, if not ending. By then many companies had acquired substantial positions in a number of plays and realized that it would take strong capital to drill and prove their positions in each of them. It triggered a major consolidation of positions and reshuffling of assets. I was able to capitalize on this by buying some assets from Chesapeake and all of the assets of Marathon and Marubeni as they exited the Basin.

My Exxon experience paid off in spades here. Many of the smaller independent companies in Denver did not want to touch the deal because of the involvement of Marubeni, a large Japanese conglomerate. I had learned how to work with such entities during my time in Malaysia. I had also learned how to work my way into the Marathon organization, becoming well acquainted with the senior person managing the sale. We both had big company experience and spoke the same language. He learned to trust me, and I spoke bluntly with him. In the process, I learned that they wanted to get out of the Basin with one closing and be done with it. They were not going to be concerned if they left a few scraps on the table. We structured our bid accordingly, taking the chaff with the wheat, and won their assets, beating out several larger companies who tried to cherry pick the deal. There was some scrambling around for financing, as our equity investors supported the approach, but did not have the capital to completely pull it off. On June 30, 2013, we closed the deal in Houston.

I was very pleased with this asset purchase, but I did not know how good it was until the following March, when a small publicly owned company in Denver offered us a large sum for most of these assets. I had always wanted to build up a large exploration and production company and didn't take the offer as seriously at first. However, common sense prevailed, and I accepted. This deal was closed on July 6, 2014. For the first time, Patsy and I had come into some serious money. This left us with a net worth nearly ten times what it had been when I left Exxon.

During all of this, Patsy's health was in the back of our minds. Little things continued to build on her falling episodes. She had difficulty getting up from a chair, loss of balance, and sometimes slight difficulty with speech. We wondered if they were marks of age or something much worse, possibly a small stroke? We knew it was time to see a specialist.

After searching in both Houston and Denver, we found a neurologist, and he diagnosed Patsy with amyloid angiopathy, resulting in Parkinsonism. We were relieved to at least have a concrete diagnosis. The doctor explained that the MRI was showing buildup of the protein amyloid in the area of the brain where Parkinson's is most closely connected. Patsy's movement problems were related to Parkinson's in that way, but she was not exhibiting the standard Parkinson's symptoms. The recommendation was exercise and a small daily dose of Sinemet.

Sinemet, a dopamine drug, is the only prescription known for Parkinson's patients. Unfortunately, it is prescribed as a way to manage the symptoms and cannot cure the underlying disease. We began the Sinemet dosage in 2014, increased our walking together, and Patsy began attending a specialty exercise program several times a week. Over the course of 2014, her symptoms seemed to stabilize. Being so close to her, I did not fully appreciate how much she had already deteriorated. Her mental faculties were still fairly sharp, and she was able to walk, and in fact even drove herself to the exercise classes. But, on a number of occasions, I did get questions like, "Is your wife okay?" Or even, "What is wrong with your wife?" My mind was too busy doing its best to pretend that all was well, and we would walk our way out of this.

On one particularly prescient incident, we went to a Zac Brown concert on the south side of Denver in the summer of 2014. One of the attendees asked me about Patsy's health and then said, "My late wife had a similar thing, and you had better watch it, as her mental health begins to decline." I brushed the comment off, as I couldn't really do anything with it.

*****

During the late summer and early fall of 2014, two forces were coming together in my mind on a totally different front. One was that I had tremendous gratitude for and loyalty to Franklin and Marshall College because of the great boost that it had given me on my professional career. The other was my Pennsylvania Dutch tradition of "paying my debts." From the time we had some discretionary money, I had thought that I would like to give back to F&M. Not just in general but to two entities that had helped me—the geosciences and the wrestling team. A number of years earlier, a friend of mine and I had started a special fund for the geosciences, which allowed the department to sponsor student research, send students on field trips, publish newsletters, and do other things not in the department budget.

When I graduated from F&M and headed to Texas, one of the geology professors, Dr. Don Wise, had said to me, "Well, Dave, if I hear that you've gone to work for an oil company, I'll know that you've sold your soul to the devil." Fast-forward about ten years, and I'm sitting at my desk at Exxon when I get a call from Don Wise. Exxon, at great expense, had created a map called the Tectonic Map of the World. It showed every significant feature of the earth's crust: faults, mountain ranges, mid-ocean ridges, and so forth. After a few years of using it for their purposes, Exxon had determined that it no longer had proprietary use, and they donated it to the American Association of Petroleum Geologists (AAPG) for them to sell for fundraising purposes. The AAPG sold it for $1,000 per copy. So Don was on the phone saying, "Dave, don't you work for Exxon? We'd like to have one of those Tectonic Maps, but we can't afford the $1,000. Could you get Exxon to give it to us for nothing?" Well, I couldn't help but tease him about coming to the devil for help now that he needed something! A few alumni chipped in and bought the map and had it framed for display in the Geoscience Department, where professors and students still use it today. This was the first contribution to what was to become the Geoscience Founders Society. One debt paid.

How to pay back the wrestling program had yet to hit me, when in 2013, I read an article in the *Wall Street Journal* about Stanford's athletic program. Every one of their athletic teams was funded by an endowment. It eliminated any question about cutting the budget for the athletic programs. At the time, a lot of wrestling programs around the US were being cut as a way for colleges to save money and comply with Federal Title IX requirements dictating a balance of programs between men and women. I had always been proud of the fact that I had wrestled at F&M. It was the only Division I athletic program at an otherwise Division III school. After reading this article, I thought that it would be a good idea to endow the wrestling program at F&M to ensure its continuity. At a meeting with the president of F&M in late 2013, I floated the idea with him. His response was, "Well, that is fine, but it will cost you five million dollars." I filed that away, not having an extra $5 million lying around anywhere.

By the summer of 2014, it seemed that the required amount might be in reach and that, given the tax situation, it would only be a net $3 million if we gave it in the same calendar year as the deal with Marathon. One big question—what would Patsy think of this idea? I knew that she was under stress because of her physical difficulties, but furthermore, here was the lady who deliberated for some time before putting a quarter in the slot machine when we were on our honeymoon. She did not like to part with her money. It took several weeks of lively debate and careful examination of our brokerage accounts for her to be sure. Finally, she said, "If that is what you really want to do, I am not going to stand in your way." It was hard for her, but she did it, and I am so glad she did, as it was one of the last significant decisions we made as a couple.

In the meantime, I had been nominated and selected to be on the board of trustees of Franklin and Marshall College. This was an honor for me, and Patsy was thrilled about it as well. In recognition of my wrestling endowment gift, F&M gave a dinner in my honor, to be attended by the other trustees, the wrestling team and friends. Patsy had a grand time at the dinner, sitting beside President Porterfield. Later, he said to me that he could tell how much she was enjoying it because at several times during key parts of the program, she would reach over and put her hand on his. I still don't know whether she thought it was worth $5 million, but she had a good time and was taking genuine pride in our accomplishments.

My debt to F&M was paid. But my life's biggest challenge was about to begin. Starting in December 2014, my total focus was on taking care of my Patsy and nursing her back to health. It was a challenge I would never conquer, and my failure was devastating.

17

Blindsided

The doctor's diagnosis had given Patsy and me the means to create a treatment plan and gave us a renewed focus on her health. The walking and exercise classes were helping, and no new episodes were cropping up.

Up until late October 2014, Patsy had been driving her own car. Maybe she should not have been, but she loved the independence, and while I was busy doing what I could for her, I was also pretending that nothing was really wrong. We were going to exercise our way out of this. We continued our long walks but added a convertible walker so that she could better maintain her balance and also sit down to rest when she needed. Hannah, our twenty-pound cocker spaniel was always with us. We would go for about two miles, sometimes taking two or more hours. Oh, how I wish we could still be doing that!

Over the last two weeks of December, Patsy's condition deteriorated rapidly. Suddenly, on bad days, she could not get up or walk without assistance. I had to help her to the bathroom, brush her teeth before going to bed, and dress her. She began to have extreme difficulty speaking, and even more alarming was that she was having trouble understanding what I was saying to her. Her cognitive abilities were starting to deteriorate at the rate of her physical abilities.

We had recently hired an Alabama woman named Carol to help Patsy with the cooking and the housework. With this rapid decline, she offered to help out more, and I knew that the situation was soon going to require around the clock care. I was going to help Patsy however I could, but I also understood that I should not be her full-time caretaker. My employees depended on me to keep the business going. If I stepped down at this point, I think it would have folded. The recent experience of a friend from Houston was also floating in my head. He quit his job to devote himself full-time to caring for his wife and died soon after she did. We worked out a schedule where I took care of Patsy in the mornings, evenings, and weekends. I cut down my hours at work to make sure that I could be there for as much of what was happening as I could.

I called Carol, and she offered to care for Patsy during the day and asked if she could split the caregiver chores with another woman who was looking for that type of work. Her name was Ira, one of a large contingent of Russians in Denver. Natasha and Sandy came on board soon after, and eventually we had a retinue of ladies helping out. These caregivers helped me create a support system for Patsy, allowing me to maintain some semblance of normalcy and probably saving my life. Patsy loved all of her caregivers; Carol and Ira remained her main two caregivers throughout the next two years.

As the events of December 2014 unfolded and continued through the early part of the following year, it was clear that the time for pretending was over. For the first time, I was scared.

18

The Verdict

I was foolish for thinking we had this thing handled in the summer of 2014. After the December downturn, I insisted that Patsy's treating neurologist direct me to another specialist. He suggested the Rocky Mountain Movement Disorder Center. It took an inordinate amount of time to get an appointment, but finally we had one—Thursday, June 11, 2015. I will never forget that day. We spent about two hours with Dr. Kumar. He had Patsy undergo many physical and mental tests before coming back to us with his diagnosis. He warned us that he did not like to sugarcoat things, and I would say that that was an understatement. By the time he was finished talking to us, we felt that we should stop by the cemetery on the way home from his office. His diagnosis was multiple system atrophy (MSA) *and* Alzheimer's. The MSA was a new one on us. He gave us some literature and let us know that the average life expectancy was seven years with no existing cure. There wasn't much a treatment plan for us, but he did increase Patsy's dosage of Sinemet. I didn't agree with his Alzheimer's diagnosis, and I still feel that way. My father had Alzheimer's, and although I clearly recognized Patsy's impaired cognitive abilities, this seemed distinctly different and would remain so.

While there was definitely a progressive cognitive impairment that accompanied Patsy's MSA, it was different in significant ways. Patsy lost the ability to read a book. The doctor's gave her simple tests which she was not able to accomplish: draw the face of a clock showing three o'clock, multiply five times twenty-five, and so forth. Up until the end, though, on her good days, she had a sense of where she was and what her surroundings were and could recognize people. In her final days, she recognized when she was home and the comfort that brought to her settled right into her bones.

We drove home in a state of shock. When we got home, I did not know what to say. My first reaction was to reassure her, as I would continue to do for the next year and a half. "We had licked the MAC, and we were going to lick this thing too." I asked her how she was feeling, and she said, "I have no regrets. I've had a good life. I'm just glad that no matter what happens to me, you'll be able to be here for Lisa." My heart absolutely broke.

In the days that followed, I wanted to make damn sure we knew what we had here. I wanted the best care possible and scoured the Internet for the world's top doctors in this field. I wanted a second opinion on the diagnosis, and then I wanted to figure out the best possible treatment. I made it clear to the neurologists that we would go anywhere in the world, and the response was unanimous. Dr. Joe Jenkovic, at the Baylor College of Medicine in Houston, had written a book that all the other neurologists used on this subject. I managed to get an appointment with Dr. Jenkovic on July 23 at 9:30 a.m.

Dr. Jenkovic had six other doctors on his staff. One of them, Dr. Tarakot, spent about an hour with us, listening to the story and asking questions. When Dr. Jenkovic came in and asked his assistant why we were there, he said, "For confirmation of an MSA diagnosis." Dr. Jenkovic's immediate response was, "Well, that can't be. She is too old." Patsy was seventy. Apparently, his experience was that people almost always contracted this in their fifties or midsixties. My heart jumped with hope. He spent another forty-five minutes asking Patsy questions, giving her tests and asking me questions. He had her walk back and forth in a room, sit down and stand up, and captured her physical movements on film to examine later. I was getting my hopes up. Dr. Jenkovic was a dapper man with a regal and pleasant air about him. At the end, he said, "I hate to confirm MSA because it is so devastating, but we have this and this," and he continued to list all the symptoms. Then he did something I've never had a doctor do. He turned to me and said, "What do you think?" By this time, I'd researched the disease to a fair extent, and so I just said, as much as I did not want to believe it, "Well, the symptoms all seem to point that way." He replied, "They do indeed."

Dr. Jenkovic did bring a small bright spot into all of this. He confirmed that Patsy had a certain amount of cognitive impairment typical of Parkinson's, but she did not have Alzheimer's.

We left Baylor armed with an increased dosage of Sinemet, new medication to enhance her chronically low blood pressure, an anxiety medication to counter some of the possible effects of the other medications, and several other prescriptions I will not belabor here. The increase in the dosage of Sinemet made Patsy drowsy and changed her sleep patterns to the point where she slept most of the twenty-four-hour day. Fortunately, when Patsy was awake, she was pretty alert but continued to have difficulty speaking. What I remember most about the summer of 2015 was going to speech and physical therapy at Rose Medical outpatient. Rose had a heated therapy pool that Patsy loved. She would do arm exercises and walk around in the water. When I stopped by to see her in action, I invariably got a big smile. She tried her best in speech therapy, but progress was elusive. The disease was progressing so rapidly that her efforts could not keep up with it.

19

MSA

Multiple system atrophy (MSA) is not Parkinson's. However, it is often first diagnosed as Parkinson's because they have similar "first-sign" symptoms of trouble with motor function, balance, and coordination. Comparisons are frequently drawn between the two diseases, as they originate in the same part of the brain and are also both connected to the production of alpha-synuclien (a protein) and dopamine (a neurotransmitter).

The Mayo Clinic defines multiple system atrophy "as a rare neurological disorder that impairs your body's involuntary (autonomic) functions, including blood pressure, heart rate, bladder function, and digestion." It was formerly called Shy-Drager syndrome after the two physicians who first described it, Dr. Milton Shy and Dr. Glenn Drager. Far fewer people are affected by MSA than Parkinson's, so the amount of research surrounding it is smaller. However, The MSA Coalition and the Baylor School of Medicine are excellent resources. The current body of research has found no cause or cure. Treatment for MSA includes medications and lifestyle changes to help manage symptoms. It progresses far faster than Parkinson's and will eventually lead to death.

There is a growing body of evidence suggesting a connection with the development of diseases like Parkinson's and MSA and the gut. Several recent studies lead me to believe that there are factors in Patsy's medical history—genetic predispositions aside—that played a role in the onset of this disease.

The first person who ever mentioned the "gut-brain connection" to me was a friend of mine in Denver, Pat Broe. Pat is an investor with both a personal and professional interest in newly developing medical trends. He first introduced me to probiotics for Patsy when he heard of her condition and our search for treatments.

My interest in the subject was further piqued when I learned of Dr. Joan Fallon's autism research. I met Joan on the board of trustees of Franklin and Marshall College. Joan was a pediatrician for twenty-five years and is currently researching the cause(s) of autism. The amount of strife it caused in the lives of her young patients and, not insignificantly, their parents propelled her into this field. In searching her patients for a common thread, Dr. Fallon discovered that many of them had a self-restricted diet. They did not like to eat protein. This discovery led Joan to her own gut-brain connection. She determined that these children lacked a critical enzyme, cryptomysin, in their digestive tract.

Cryptomysin is secreted by the pancreas and vital to the digestion of protein. Protein is critical to the body because it helps create amino acids, which are an essential part of a healthy neurological system. Scientists have connected amino acids to the creation of crucial brain neurotransmitters like serotonin and dopamine. Dopamine is a key neurotransmitter for controlling motor function. A broken link in this chain can have serious repercussions in the body's systems.

Dr. Fallon sees the potential for similar or related gut-brain connections in other severe neurological diseases, including Parkinson's, cystic fibrosis, schizophrenia, and addiction.

In a report from the Michael J. Fox Foundation, the protein alpha-synuclein, which clumps in the brains of Parkinson's patients, is also commonly first found on the nerves controlling the intestines. This may be why intestinal dysfunction, including constipation, is a common precursor to the actual onset of Parkinson's. Little is known about the function of alpha-synuclein in healthy humans. Scientists have only been able to discover that it's clumping or abnormal formation is usually a precursor to Parkinson's and MSA. Its pre-disease function is unknown.

Dr. Scheperjan, the researcher quoted in the Michael J. Fox report, also reports that Parkinson's patients have lower levels of the bacteria prevotella in their intestines. Prevotella aids in the creation of the vitamins thiamine and folate. Thiamine is key in nerve, muscle, and heart function; and folate is key in producing new cells. Studies have shown that there are subtle differences in the bacteria types between people with various types of Parkinson's. Researchers have just scratched the surface of the findings in this area.

In April 2017, five months after Patsy's death, I had a Eureka moment. I've since wondered why it was so long coming, but with her illness and my months of grief, clarity was a rare thing. I had a minor ear infection and went to a walk-in medical clinic to have it looked at. The attending physician recommended a dose of antibiotics. I asked whether there was any downside to taking the antibiotics. Her response: "Well, in someone seventy years old, this will kill some of your gut bacteria and could result in diarrhea." Then it hit me.

After Patsy was diagnosed with MAC in 2010, the doctors got rid of her condition with a strong cocktail of three antibiotics that were used for months. As I further researched and thought back over Patsy's medical situation, I realized that she had a much longer history with antibiotics. Patsy suffered from chronic sinus infections, and for years she took antibiotics to cure these. She frequently travelled with a dose of antibiotics in the event that an infection occurred unexpectedly while we were out of town.

I believe that Patsy's long-term use of antibiotics to cure the MAC may have triggered the onset of her MSA a few years later. The situation may have even been exacerbated by her antibiotic use over the previous years. I believe that research in the coming years will further confirm the gut-brain connection. I think that a new area of concern will be more careful prescription of antibiotics and ways to counteract their adverse impact on the digestive system. It may also turn out that the lack of cryptomysin in infant's guts is related to antibiotic use or perhaps indirect antibiotic implications from non-organic foods, especially in chicken, pork, and beef.

20

One More Trip

The son of some very good friends of ours from Houston, Parrish Chin, was getting married on September 18, 2015, in New York City. Patsy and Debbe Chin, Parrish's mother, were extremely close; and we loved the entire family. Patsy very much wanted to go, and so I said we'd go. I had made the decision a few years before, because of the complications of our life, that access to private air travel would be one luxury I could justify. It paid off here, because I certainly could not have made this trek otherwise. Lisa accompanied us, and we all had a grand time. She was in a wheelchair most of the time and continued to have difficulty speaking. But she was into everything in spirit and would occasionally hop up and start walking around without assistance. I am still so glad we went on this trip.

About a week after returning to Denver, I came home after work to take over from the caregiver when I noticed Patsy distinctly wheezing. I took her to the emergency room immediately, and it was determined that she had aspiration pneumonia; the first of several she would contract over the next year. Patsy's respiratory system was slowly getting weaker, and she remained in the hospital for about ten days. One night, her condition deteriorated to the point of a code blue and every doctor and nurse on staff rallied into the room to resuscitate her. She made it and came home from the hospital weaker, but she regained some strength after a few weeks. After this, we had some good times together, going to movies and eating out. She really seemed to be perking up.

Patsy had always put on a grand Christmas, but this year, she was weak and not in a mood to get the house overly decorated. However, she still loved to shop, so I would put her in the wheelchair and wheeled her around the Cherry Creek Mall. The clerks recognized her at all the stores she loved, chatting her up and seeing how she was doing. She had a big smile for all of them, and it was lovely for me to watch.

During that winter and the following spring, things were fairly stable. Patsy went to her speech and pool therapy several times a week. On March 17, 2016, Joe and Susan Hull, very good friends of ours from Texas, were celebrating their fiftieth wedding anniversary in Marble Falls, Texas. We both wanted to go and celebrate with them. I suggested to the Hull's that Patsy and I come by their house to say hello, prior to joining the large gathering, and this proved to be the right decision. Patsy perked up and was even able to question Susan about her many travels (while leaving Joe home to work). The celebration itself was a bit difficult for us as Patsy's difficulties speaking had not improved, and she needed to stay seated the entire time. We went to see Dr. Jenkovic on April 27. This was the last trip that Patsy would make.

21

The Sudden Turn

May 27, 2016, is a day burned into my memory like no other. Two days earlier, Lisa, Patsy, and I had gone to dinner at Piatti's Italian Restaurant in Denver to celebrate Patsy's seventy-first birthday. Patsy, at this point, was confined to a wheelchair, and she continued to have difficulty talking—but her mind was still very aware of her surroundings. As she sat in the living room in her wheelchair before dinner, she perked up and in a clear and chipper voice said, "Well, I wonder what we'll be doing say, two years from now." It still feels as though she said it yesterday. It showed me that she was hopeful but understood her situation, so she dared go out two years but not ten. I almost cried, but tears are not for birthdays!

Dinner was lovely, and Patsy really seemed to have a good time. Several other diners, recognizing the birthday celebration, came by to wish her well. Unfortunately, her condition precluded any long conversations. At the end of dinner, I wheeled her to the car and, in a routine that we had down to an art, helped her into the front seat and put her wheelchair in the back. We had always loved riding in the car together, and I sensed that even this short drive brought back memories of a number of long road trips we had taken over our life together.

Friday, May 27, 2016, at 11:00 a.m., I was sitting at the desk in my office in downtown Denver when I received a phone call. It was Patsy's caregiver Ira. "Patsy is having convulsions and screaming. She is in a lot of pain, and I can't do anything to help her." I immediately called 911 and met the paramedics at our condominium. The doctors at the emergency room were in contact with her primary Parkinson's physician in Houston. They determined that this reaction was not a normal feature of her illness but were not sure what could have brought it on. She was admitted to the intensive care unit. They prescribed Ativan for the convulsions, and it worked, but it put her out. She slept the remainder of the day Friday and most of Saturday. By Sunday morning, I was becoming frantic about giving her the Parkinson's medications. Her nurse and I decided that we should try to give them to her. Unfortunately, she aspirated and then was in even worse shape, as she developed aspiration pneumonia. She was given antibiotics and fluids intravenously for several days.

By Wednesday, June 1, she still was not able to eat or drink anything orally. The doctors asked to speak with me. We had a serious conference in which they described her situation and recommended she undergo PEG, or percutaneous endoscopic gastronomy. It is a surgical procedure that places a feeding tube into the abdomen so that liquid nourishment and medications can be directly fed into the stomach. Although I have since learned that this is all a well-established and common practice, I was entering a whole new world. The tube would allow Patsy to be fed without the risk of aspiration, to say nothing of the fact that her muscles for swallowing were weakened significantly.

Although we had been travelling down a difficult path for a couple of years now, it wasn't until this moment when I was really hit with an overwhelming awareness of what I'll call the dignity factor, a matter on which I will write more later. Patsy had been a beautiful and athletic woman in her prime. Now I was being asked to allow the implantation of a tube so that she could be artificially fed. I asked what the alternative was. Without it, she would slowly starve to death. As much as I hated to see her in such a feeble state, I definitely wanted her with me. It might be a temporary thing, they said, until she regains her strength. Hope springs eternal.

Now that Patsy could take nourishment and her medications, she slowly gained some strength back. The physical therapists worked with her on range of motion in her arms and legs. But now another reality was facing us. Patsy had lost about twenty pounds and was down to a frail eighty-five pounds. Although the convulsions were gone, her large leg muscles had contracted, and she was in a type of permanent fetal position. My Patsy was now bedridden. I had known for over a year that this day would likely come—but nonetheless, it devastated me. When Patsy was originally admitted to the emergency room, she was also diagnosed with a urinary tract infection (UTI). Although none of the physicians would give me a definitive answer, it was clear that the UTI, in conjunction with her underlying MSA, had brought on this rapid and disheartening deterioration of her physical condition.

By Monday, June 6, the physicians determined that Patsy was stable enough to go home. On Tuesday morning, a visiting nurse came by around noon to check on her. I had felt very uneasy all morning as her breathing was labored, and she seemed to be very uncomfortable, possibly in pain. She could not talk at this point. The nurse examined her briefly and looked at me and said, "This lady is sick and needs to be in the hospital." She called 911 for me.

Because of her labored breathing, the paramedics placed a breathing tube down Patsy's throat while in the ambulance. The nurse's warned me prior to my seeing her, and I am glad they did. Once again, she was admitted to the emergency room. Over the next few days, the doctors repositioned the breathing tube to her nose and put her on a ventilator. After four or five days of weaning off the ventilator, they determined that she could breathe on her own, and we all waited anxiously for the grand experiment. The tube was removed, and Patsy breathed fine for about thirty minutes, at which time she began panting and heaving to breathe. The tube had to be quickly reinserted.

When Patsy was readmitted to the hospital with breathing problems, a doctor from National Jewish Health, renowned for its respiratory specialization, began consulting on the case. She had mentioned to me soon after readmittance that a trach might be necessary. I thought that she was mistaken and refused to let my mind even consider it. To my chagrin, the doctors soon asked for a consultation and recommended that a trach be inserted. In my desperation and naiveté, I again asked what the alternative was. Again, there was no real choice, but there was still the possibility that this would be temporary.

Patsy remained in the ICU but seemed to be making progress with her breathing. Within a week or two, she was able to breathe through a "trach collar," without the ventilator, for increasing amounts of time. After about two weeks with this, she could maintain it for around an hour. I spent most of my time with her, only leaving to get meals or a cup of coffee.

For the first week, I spent my nights at the hospital, sleeping on a fold out bed in Patsy's room. After a few weeks, Patsy was able to breathe without the ventilator, and I would take her for excursions about the grounds in her wheelchair. The nurses insisted on attending us for safety, but sometimes we managed to sneak away on our own. She loved being out in the sunshine and fresh air. Her strength would wane from day to day, but on good days, Patsy was alert and able to sit in her chair. Physical therapists came by to stretch her legs and arms. We even had some modest success with a speech therapist and would both get excited when she could say a few words around the trach.

It was now about the middle of June. Several months earlier, we had received an invitation to the wedding of one of Patsy's and my favorite nephews, Brad Hayes. When I read the invitation to Patsy, she said, "I want to go." The wedding was to be at the end of June in Jackson, Tennessee. I told the doctors at Rose Medical about the event; and Dr. Schwartz, her primary physician in the ICU, made it his mission to try to get her there. However, given that she had a new trach, they would not release her to travel without a nurse in attendance. Finding such a nurse proved to be daunting, and in the end impossible.

One of the many things I learned through this ordeal is that nurses are licensed by state, and finding a nurse licensed in both Colorado and Tennessee was like the proverbial needle in a haystack, but you weren't even sure the needle would be in there. During this entire time in the ICU, Patsy remained cheerful, and despite her limited speaking ability, she made the doctors and nurses feel good with her infectious smile. As an indication of the effect she had on people, one of the doctors, upon hearing about my troubles finding a nurse for our travels, said that if we could not find one she would go with us! I was bowled over with gratitude and amazement. I will never forget Dr. Sergew's gesture of kindness. As it turned out, Patsy, despite some improvement, was just not strong enough by the end of June to make the trip; and we decided against it. Brad and Melissa were so impressed with Patsy's desire to be there that they made the trip to Denver two months later to see her in person.

At the end of June, the doctors in the emergency room informed me that Patsy, having been there almost a month, would have to be moved. They would not allow her to go home directly with a new trach but recommended an "acute care facility." There were only three to choose from in Denver, and I selected Kindred, a few miles away from my office. The physician in charge was known for his ability to care for trach patients. Patsy was gaining strength every day, and even making progress in her speech. The physicians at Rose said that this step was only a precaution and after "about a week" she would be able to go home. Five months later, I was finally able to bring Patsy home.

The stay at Kindred was worse than any nightmare I could have ever imagined. The day-by-day series of events is too painful for me to write about, so I will describe certain aspects of those long months. Our routine. I was there for all of Patsy's first month in the ICU. As the weeks ticked by, I knew that for both my mental and physical health, I needed to create a routine outside of the hospital cafeteria and coffee machine. I needed to go back to work.

I would get up around 5:30 each morning and make it to the hospital by 7:15 a.m. After checking with the nurses to see how Patsy did through the night, I would talk with her on the mornings when she was awake and alert or otherwise just stay with her, holding her hand and praying for her to recover. When her caregiver arrived at about 8:00 a.m., I would go to the office and come back around noon for lunch. During this time, I would talk to the caregiver about how Patsy was doing and then talk to Patsy. Some days, she would be awake but not alert enough to let me know that she was aware of things. On other days, she would be asleep. I would return again in the evening around five thirty and stay until eight thirty or nine o'clock, grabbing a bite to eat along the way as I could. I spent all day Saturdays, Sundays, and holidays with her. When she was not awake, I would sit there and hold her hand, praying for her recovery. When she was awake, I would read books to her, which she absolutely loved. During the summer and early fall of 2016, I read four books to her (Dave's books on tape!); Bill O'Reilly's *Killing Patton*, *Killing Kennedy*, and *Killing the Rising Sun*; as well as Brian Kilmeade's *Thomas Jefferson* and the *Barbary Pirates*.

Patsy loved history, especially books about the Second World War, where her father fought in North Africa as a member of the

Army Air Corps. In the late summer of 2014, I first became aware of Patsy's deteriorating cognitive abilities when she would go out onto the patio with a copy of *Killing Patton*. She would come in an hour or so later, pretending to have read this whole time, but I noticed that the bookmark kept staying in the same place. Broke my heart for her.

Soon after arriving at Kindred, Patsy suffered another bout of aspiration pneumonia. This, of course, involved another round of antibiotics and set her back several weeks. More than this, it seemed to set her on a downward spiral from which she never really recovered. We talked about putting her in a wheelchair and taking her for "walks" as we had done at Rose. Unfortunately, her breathing kept declining, and after several months, the doctors gave up hope of weaning her off the ventilator. A special new type of PEG tube was inserted into her stomach to try to minimize the chance of aspiration pneumonia. This seemed to work pretty well. However, she contracted another UTI soon after recovering from the aspiration pneumonia. It took an especially long time to treat and each of these episodes left her weaker and weaker.

One Saturday morning in September, I arrived at the hospital to see the head nurse frantically attending to Patsy preparing to take her to the ICU inside the acute care hospital. Her blood pressure had dropped to dangerously low levels—about 60/40. She was having fever spikes up to 103 degrees, and they were concerned about her going septic. The ICU in Kindred was an especially inhospitable looking place. It was a multiple bedroom on the top floor of what felt like a converted attic. After a week or so in ICU, the doctors concluded that Patsy's spikes in temperature were most likely being caused by the UTI antibiotics and promptly took her off them. Sure enough, she slowly got better and after another two weeks or so was proclaimed ready to move out of the ICU. During her stay in the ICU, she had largely been in a coma or near coma, and I was overwhelmed when she came around and got out of the ICU.

Those five months were a period of great stress. Some of the causes were obvious. I had brought Patsy there thinking—hoping—that this would be temporary. That we would be home soon. That none of this was happening. Her condition continued to deteriorate.

Every moment I spent outside the walls of her room, I wondered how Patsy was going to be the next time I stepped through the door. Will she be awake and alert with one of those big smiles? Or will I have missed that and I find her barely there, or sleeping? On top of this, I was in a constant battle with the nurses and doctors.

A good example of this was the "thirty-degree guideline." The head doctor instructed the nurses to keep the head of Patsy's bed at thirty degrees for several reasons. It reduces the risk of aspiration, which could trigger another battle with pneumonia, and it also helps regulate blood pressure in Patsy's head as MSA negatively affects its regulation throughout the body. Oftentimes, I would arrive, and the bed would be at only twenty degrees. I would not only complain to the nurse but to the head nurse. They would put up signs for the next shift. Finally, there would be signs all over the room: "Keep top of bed at thirty degrees." I would similarly raise hell when I'd arrive and she would be wet, not having been changed. Some of the nurses really cared and tried hard, others not so much. I blacklisted two nurses from caring for Patsy. The doctors were only a little better. One benefit of being at the hospital so much was that I could catch the doctors on their rounds and talk with them about Patsy. Getting them to return calls was a challenge.

The head doctor specialized in trach care and spent much of his time at the hospital. We tried several different trachs, changing one of them after I was called to the hospital in the middle of the night when her new trach was not allowing her to breath. We eventually found one that worked. The other doctors, for infectious disease, neurology, and so forth, worked at several facilities and were extremely difficult to pin down unless you caught them on their rounds at Kindred. During this entire time, I spoke regularly with Patsy's primary neurological (Parkinson's) physician at Baylor Medical in Houston. In consultation with them, we decided to do an experiment with her Parkinson's medications.

Patsy had been taking Sinemet, or carpodopa levodopa, for several years. It only manages the symptoms, and one of its main side effects is drowsiness. Patsy was taking a very high dosage, so in consultation with Baylor and Kindred, we decided to take her off

Sinemet. We wanted to see if her body could manage without it and possibly become more alert. Sure enough, she perked up again without it. This, combined with Patsy's rapid three-year decline, made me think that the Sinemet probably never worked for Patsy.

During the five months at Kindred, I spent three holidays and our thirty-eighth wedding anniversary in Patsy's room. On our first holiday, the Fourth of July, I stepped out to get a cup of coffee, and when I returned, the nurse was there, and she said, "Patsy says that you served in the military." Even with her difficulty speaking, she had managed to talk to the nurse about my military service! It had always been important to Patsy and a deep source of pride for her. Even in the depths of this disease, she was able to hold onto this, breaking my heart and keeping that little flame of hope alive. About two weeks after the Fourth, I stayed late on a Friday evening, and we watched our usual Friday evening shows—Hawaii Five O followed by Blue Bloods. When they were over, I said to Patsy, "Good night, honey. I'll see you in the morning. I love you." She responded quite audibly, around the trach, "I love you too." By this time, we had created our own system of communication through smiles, gestures, and other subtle facial and bodily movements. These were the last words I ever heard her say.

Patsy's sisters Sharon and Kathy were particularly attentive and kind during this period. About two weeks after Patsy was admitted to Rose ICU (the second week in June), they both showed up in Denver. They knew that I would be reluctant to let them see Patsy in such a condition, so they did not ask permission—they just came. I am so glad that they did. Patsy and her sisters could tell stories and laugh together like nothing I've ever seen. Sure enough, here was Patsy on her hospital bed, with a new trach, able to speak only a few words at a time; but they were howling with laughter, just as raucous as any of the old times.

22

Home at Last

After nearly six months in the hospital—one month in intensive care at Rose Medical Center in Denver and over five months at Kindred—Patsy was coming home. We were both excited. Although Patsy was at a stage in her illness where she could not talk, on good days, she could communicate very effectively with nonverbal expressions; and she had brightened up about a week earlier when one of her doctors asked if she would like to go home.

It had taken me months of preparation. Some doctors at Kindred had strongly suggested that Patsy be transferred to a nursing-home-type facility where the nurses could attend to her, but the facility was over forty-five minutes away, and I wanted to be able to get to her quickly from home or the office. A special hospital bed had been ordered, a custom wheelchair was purchased, and a cadre of nurses and caregivers were lined up to take care of her. Extensive equipment, a ventilator included, was all arranged. The front room of the house, which had been my study and our TV watching room, was commandeered. The doctors, nurses, and even Patsy's friends agreed with me—if we could just get Patsy out of the hospital and into a familiar home, she might perk up and start doing better.

Patsy clearly recognized her surroundings when we got her situated at home, and her face morphed into a much happier visage. However, on the first night home, the nurse on duty awoke me at two in the morning announcing that Patsy's feeding tube was coming out of her abdomen and she did not know how to fix it. One 911 call and an ambulance ride later, we arrived in the emergency room with Patsy, alert and smiling at the nurses. As it turned out, it was a simple procedure, and we were back home and in bed by about 4:30 a.m. However, that second day at home. Patsy did not look good and was barely awake during the day. When I came home and started talking to her, big tears began rolling down her cheeks. She had rarely cried during the last few years of her ordeal, and never tears like this. I am convinced that she knew the end was soon.

The next morning, November 17, Patsy never quite woke up. Another call to 911. The paramedics had to resuscitate her. As the paramedics put her into the ambulance, her eyes were open, and I thought she was going to come out of it. The doctors at the emergency room informed me that she was alive but in a coma. They could keep her alive with blood pressure meds, and I asked them to do so until Lisa could get there. She was out of town on a business trip. Carol and Ira, Patsy's longtime caregivers, came to the hospital, and we all watched over Patsy and waited. Lisa and Rev. Ron Pogue, our Episcopal priest, walked in together. Reverend Pogue administered the last rites, and then Lisa and I visited at length with Dr. Schwartz, a most caring and thoughtful guy. There was no hope left.

Patsy was not going to come out of her coma. Her blood pressure medication was the only thing keeping her alive, so we agreed to stop its administration. Dr. Schwartz had advised that she likely would not live through the night. The blood pressure medication stopped at 6:00 p.m. At 6:03 p.m., the nurse informed us that Patsy was gone.

*****

I have second-guessed a number of decisions made during Patsy's illness but perhaps none more than my decision to resuscitate her on the morning of her last day. However, having Lisa there and last rites administered while she was still alive was very important to me. I think it would have meant a lot to Patsy.

When we were both healthy, as we got into our fifties and sixties, Patsy would sometimes bring up the subject of where we would be buried. I would generally put off the discussion, partly because I thought we were too young to be concerned with this and partly because it took too much effort to get my head around it. When it came time to bury Patsy, I think that I made a decision, which we would have made together if we, I, had taken the time to do it. The issue of "Do Not Resuscitate" was similarly not discussed by us. Fortunately, we made living wills, which gave each person the power to make life-and-death decisions for the other.

I similarly felt that, in a progressively degenerative disease such as this, it is virtually impossible to say at what point one should "throw in the towel." Patsy was first resuscitated in a hospital a full fourteen months before she passed away. Some of those fourteen months were pure hell, but they also contain memories that I cherish and convince me it was more than worth it.

Patsy and I lived a nomadic life together. She created a home for us everywhere we went, but we didn't lay our roots down until our final years out in Houston and Denver. We held a memorial service in Denver and had her funeral and burial at St. Martin's Episcopal Church in Houston. Houston was the beginning for us and the only place our story could end. It was our home.

*****

You rarely think about the effect someone has on you in the moment. It takes time, a fair amount of candor, and the good fortune to have both. Growing up on the farm, I always knew I was loved, but it was rarely demonstrated and usually awkwardly done. Looking back, I can see that I was truly rough as a cob in our beginnings. But Patsy smoothed me out over our decades together like water lapping over stone. Her grace, beauty, and Southern charm brought a new light into my life and redefined what happiness meant to me.

Whenever someone dies, especially someone who was as well loved by so many people as Patsy, you expect to hear many kind words and accolades. The warm words and stories people told about her overwhelmed me. As the widow, I wasn't asked to say much, and as time has passed, I have been given the opportunity to look back on our life with a renewed sense of gratitude and love for this woman.

The love we shared was deep and true. It buoyed us in rough times and made the good times all the sweeter. This book is a drop in the sea of kind words and accolades I could give about Patsy. She was my Southern Belle. My Patsy. My home.

Bibliography

"LRRK2 Safety Initiative." The Michael J. Fox Foundation for Parkinson's Research | Parkinson's Disease. Accessed March 30, 2019. https://www.michaeljfox.org/understanding-parkinsons/living-with-pd/topic.php?alpha-synuclein.

"Multiple System Atrophy (MSA)." Baylor College of Medicine. Accessed March 28, 2019. https://www.bcm.edu/healthcare/care-centers/parkinsons/conditions/multiple-system-atrophy.

Lee, Kuan Yew. From Third World to First: the Singapore Story, 1965-2000: Memoirs of Lee Kuan Yew. Singapore: Marshall Cavendish Editions, 2015.

Mohamad, Mahathir bin. The Malay Dilemma. Singapore: Marshall Cavendish Editions, 2010.

"Multiple System Atrophy (MSA)." Mayo Clinic. Mayo Foundation for Medical Education and Research, June 17, 2017. https://www.mayoclinic.org/diseases-conditions/multiple-system-atrophy/symptoms-causes/syc-20356153.

"Multiple System Atrophy Overview." MSA Coalition. Accessed March 30, 2019. https://www.multiplesystematrophy.org/about-msa.

Want to Learn More about MSA?

....

Multiple System Atrophy CoalitionTM
https://www.multiplesystematrophy.org/
9935-D Rea Road, #212 Charlotte, NC 28277
Tel: (866)-737-4999
Multiple System Atrophy Trust
http://www.msatrust.org.uk
51 St Olav's Court City Business Centre Lower Road,
London SE16 2XB
Baylor College of Medicine Medical Center
https://www.bcm.edu/healthcare/care-centers/parkinsons
McNair Campus, 7200 Cambridge St., 9th Floor, Suite 9A, Houston,
    TX 77030

About the Author

....

David H. (Dave) Lehman was born and raised on a farm in Lancaster County, Pennsylvania, the son of Roy Jacob and Esther Hershey Lehman. Bob Hartman, his high school wrestling coach, got him into Franklin and Marshall College, an excellent school where he discovered the study of Geology, which was to become his passion in life. He served as a non-commissioned officer in the United States Army in Vietnam from 1969 to 1970. His degree in Geology from The University of Texas at Austin led to a distinguished career in the oil business, including 27 years with Exxon (now ExxonMobil) and subsequently in the independent oil-and-gas arena, where he has founded three successful companies.

Lehman received the inspiration for this book when, while grieving the loss of his wife, he read the book by Victor Lee Austin titled "Losing Susan: Brain Disease, the Priest's Wife, and the God Who Gives and Takes Away."

CPSIA information can be obtained
at www.ICGtesting.com
Printed in the USA
BVHW081935110721
611621BV00002B/5/J

9 781648 015601